Collins

Teacher's Guide 5

Vocabulary, Grammar and Punctuation Skills

Author: Abigail Steel

William Collins' dream of knowledge for all began with the publication of his first book in 1819.

A self-educated mill worker, he not only enriched millions of lives, but also founded a flourishing publishing house. Today, staying true to this spirit, Collins books are packed with inspiration, innovation and practical expertise. They place you at the centre of a world of possibility and give you exactly what you need to explore it.

Collins. Freedom to teach.

Published by Collins
An imprint of HarperCollins*Publishers*
The News Building
1 London Bridge Street
London
SE1 9GF

Browse the complete Collins catalogue at
www.collins.co.uk

© HarperCollins*Publishers* Limited 2017

10 9 8 7 6 5 4 3 2 1

ISBN 978-0-00-822300-7

All rights reserved. No part of this publication may be reproduced, stored in a retrieval system, or transmitted in any form by any means, electronic, mechanical, photocopying, recording or otherwise, without the prior written permission of the Publisher or a licence permitting restricted copying in the United Kingdom issues by the Copyright Licensing Agency Ltd., 90 Tottenham Court Road, London W1T 4LP.

British Library Cataloguing in Publication Data

A catalogue record for this publication is available from the British Library.

Publishing Director: Lee Newman
Publishing Manager: Helen Doran
Senior Editor: Hannah Dove
Project Manager: Emily Hooton
Author: Abigail Steel
Development Editor: Sarah Snashall
Copy-editor: Gaynor Spry
Proofreader: Trish Chapman
Cover design and artwork: Amparo Barrera and Ken Vail Graphic Design
Internal design concept: Amparo Barrera
Typesetter: Ken Vail Graphic Design
Illustrations: Aptara and QBS
Production Controller: Rachel Weaver

Printed and bound by
CPI Group (UK) Ltd, Croydon, CR0 4YY

Contents

About Treasure House 4	Review unit 2: Grammar 51
Support, embed and challenge 12	**Punctuation**
Assessment 13	Unit 1: Using commas for clearer meaning 52
Support with teaching vocabulary, grammar and punctuation 14	Unit 2: Hyphens 54
Delivering the 2014 National Curriculum for English 15	Unit 3: Brackets, dashes and commas 56
Vocabulary	Unit 4: Boundaries between clauses 58
Unit 1: Expanded noun phrases . . 21	Unit 5: Colons to introduce lists . . 60
Unit 2: Changing nouns or adjectives into verbs 24	Unit 6: Punctuating bulleted lists . . 62
Unit 3A: Verb prefixes (1) 26	Review unit 3: Punctuation 64
Unit 3B: Verb prefixes (2) 28	Photocopiable resources 65
Review unit 1: Vocabulary 30	
Grammar	
Unit 1: Formal and informal language 31	
Unit 2A: Adverbs showing possibility 33	
Unit 2B: Modal verbs showing possibility 35	
Unit 3A: Relative clauses (1) 37	
Unit 3B: Relative clauses (2) 39	
Unit 4: Linking words in paragraphs 41	
Unit 5A: Adverbials of time 43	
Unit 5B: Adverbials of place 45	
Unit 5C: Adverbials of manner . . . 47	
Unit 5D: Adverbials of number . . . 49	

About Treasure House

Treasure House is a comprehensive and flexible bank of books and online resources for teaching the English curriculum. The Treasure House series offers two different pathways: one covering each English strand discretely (Skills Focus Pathway) and one integrating texts and the strands to create a programme of study (Integrated English Pathway). This Teacher's Guide is part of the Skills Focus Pathway.

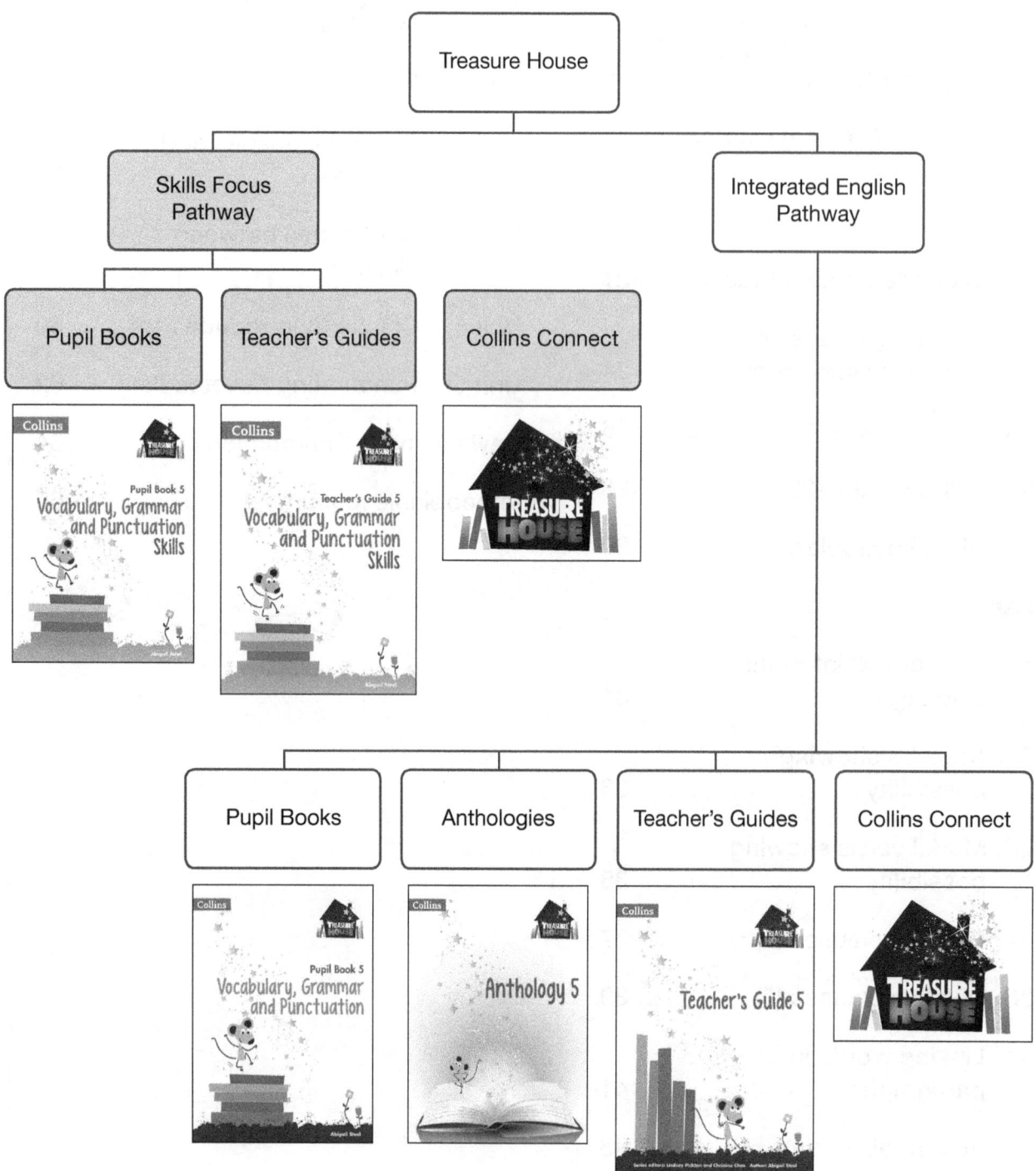

About Treasure House

1. Skills Focus

The Skills Focus Pupil Books and Teacher's Guides for all four strands (Comprehension; Spelling; Composition; and Vocabulary, Grammar and Punctuation) allow you to teach each curriculum area in a targeted way. Each unit in the Pupil Book is mapped directly to the statutory requirements of the National Curriculum. Each Teacher's Guide provides step-by-step instructions to guide you through the Pupil Book activities and digital Collins Connect resources for each competency. With a clear focus on skills and clearly-listed curriculum objectives you can select the appropriate resources to support your lessons.

  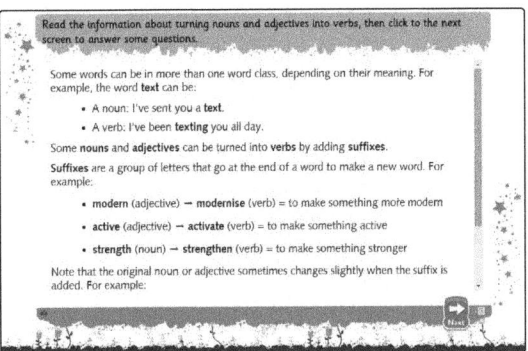

2. Integrated English

Alternatively, the Integrated English pathway offers a complete programme of genre-based teaching sequences. There is one Teacher's Guide and one Anthology for each year group. Each Teacher's Guide provides 15 teaching sequences focused on different genres of text such as fairy tales, letters and newspaper articles. The Anthologies contain the classic texts, fiction, non-fiction and poetry required for each sequence. Each sequence also weaves together all four dimensions of the National Curriculum for English – Comprehension; Spelling; Composition; and Vocabulary, Grammar and Punctuation – into a complete English programme. The Pupil Books and Collins Connect provide targeted explanation of key points and practice activities organised by strand. This programme provides 30 weeks of teaching inspiration.

   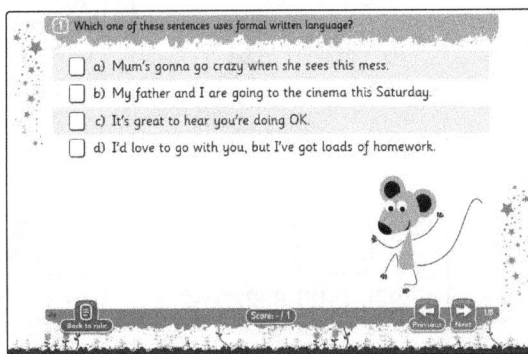

Other components

Handwriting Books, Handwriting Workbooks, Word Books and the online digital resources on Collins Connect are suitable for use with both pathways.

About Treasure House

Treasure House Skills Focus Teacher's Guides

Year	Comprehension	Composition	Vocabulary, Grammar and Punctuation	Spelling
1	978-0-00-822290-1	978-0-00-822302-1	978-0-00-822296-3	978-0-00-822308-3
2	978-0-00-822291-8	978-0-00-822303-8	978-0-00-822297-0	978-0-00-822309-0
3	978-0-00-822292-5	978-0-00-822304-5	978-0-00-822298-7	978-0-00-822310-6
4	978-0-00-822293-2	978-0-00-822305-2	978-0-00-822299-4	978-0-00-822311-3
5	978-0-00-822294-9	978-0-00-822306-9	978-0-00-822300-7	978-0-00-822312-0
6	978-0-00-822295-6	978-0-00-822307-6	978-0-00-822301-4	978-0-00-822313-7

About Treasure House

Inside the Skills Focus Teacher's Guides

The teaching notes in each unit in the Teacher's Guide provide you with subject information or background, a range of whole class and differentiated activities including photocopiable resource sheets and links to the Pupil Book and the online Collins Connect activities.

Each **Overview** provides clear objectives for each lesson tied into the new curriculum, links to the other relevant components and a list of any additional resources required.

Teaching overview provides a brief introduction to the specific concept or rule and some pointers on how to approach it.

Support, embed & challenge supports a mastery approach with activities provided at three levels.

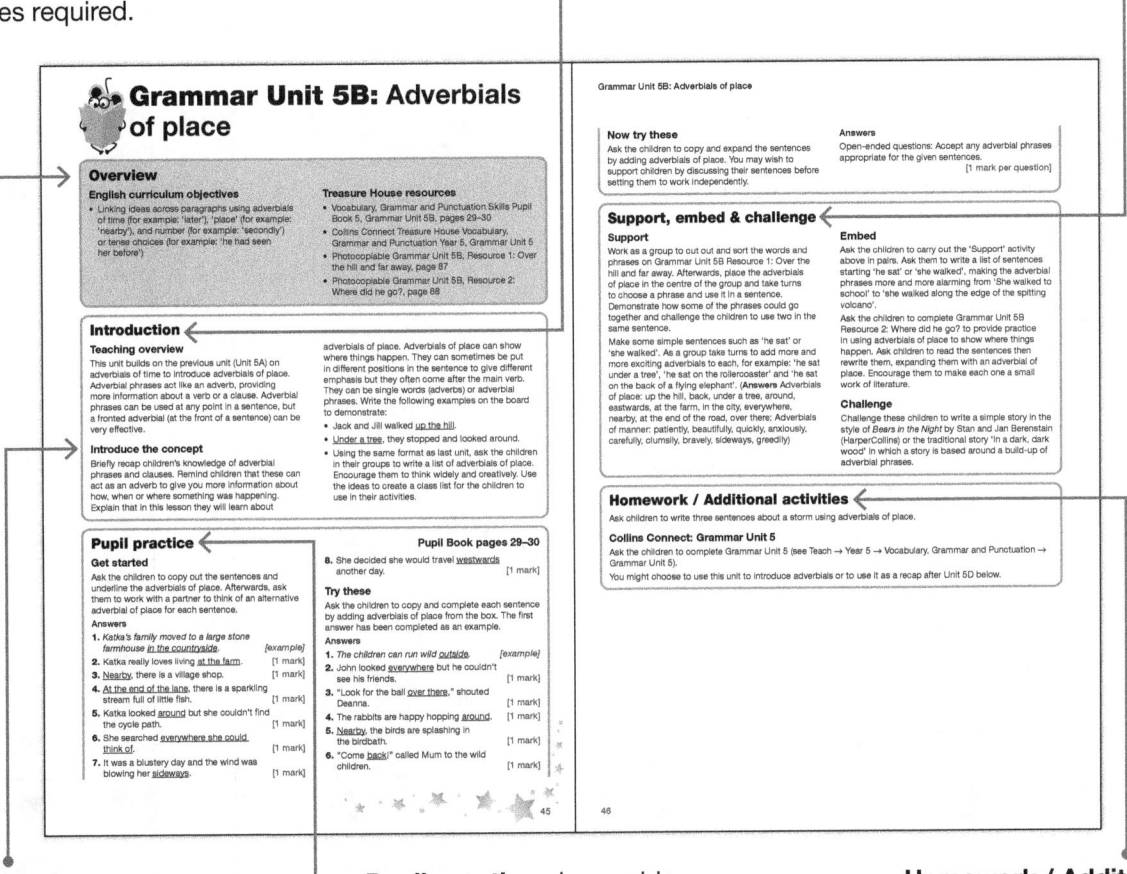

Introduce the concept provides 5–10 minutes of preliminary discussion points or class/group activities to get the pupils engaged in the lesson focus and set out any essential prior learning.

Pupil practice gives guidance and the answers to each of the three sections in the Pupil Book: *Get started*, *Try these* and *Now try these*.

Homework / Additional activities lists ideas for classroom or homework activities, and relevant activities from Collins Connect.

Two photocopiable **resource** worksheets per unit provide extra practice of the specific lesson concept. They are designed to be used with the activities in support, embed or challenge sections.

7

About Treasure House

Treasure House Skills Focus Pupil Books

There are four Skills Focus Pupil Books for each year group, based on the four dimensions of the National Curriculum for English: Comprehension; Spelling; Composition; and Vocabulary, Grammar and Punctuation. The Pupil Books provide a child-friendly introduction to each subject and a range of initial activities for independent pupil-led learning. A Review unit for each term assesses pupils' progress.

Year	Comprehension	Composition	Vocabulary, Grammar and Punctuation	Spelling
1	978-0-00-823634-2	978-0-00-823646-5	978-0-00-823640-3	978-0-00-823652-6
2	978-0-00-823635-9	978-0-00-823647-2	978-0-00-823641-0	978-0-00-823653-3
3	978-0-00-823636-6	978-0-00-823648-9	978-0-00-823642-7	978-0-00-823654-0
4	978-0-00-823637-3	978-0-00-823649-6	978-0-00-823643-4	978-0-00-823655-7
5	978-0-00-823638-0	978-0-00-823650-2	978-0-00-823644-1	978-0-00-823656-4
6	978-0-00-823639-7	978-0-00-823651-9	978-0-00-823645-8	978-0-00-823657-1

About Treasure House

Inside the Skills Focus Pupil Books
Comprehension

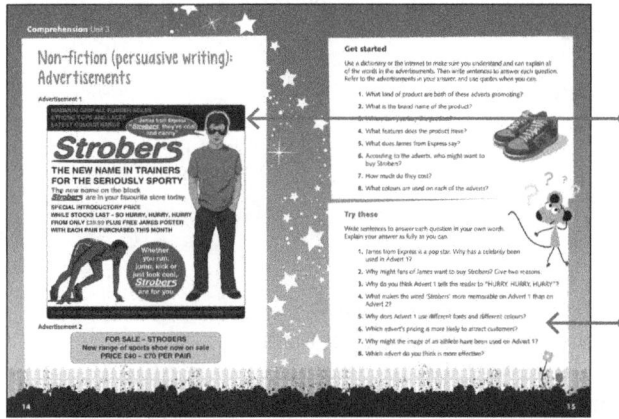

Includes high-quality text extracts covering poetry, prose, traditional tales, playscripts and non-fiction.

Pupils retrieve and record information, learn to draw inferences from texts and increase their familiarity with a wide range of literary genres.

Composition

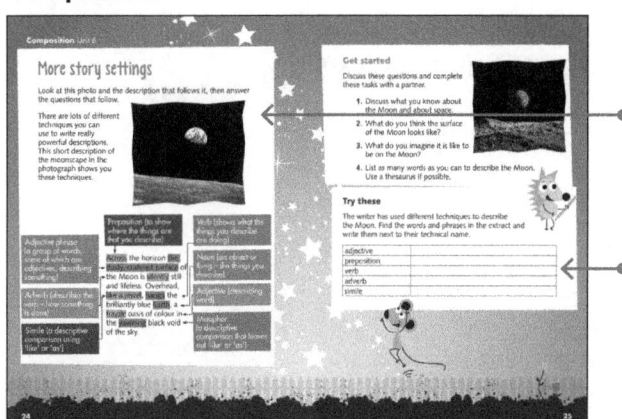

Includes high-quality, annotated text extracts as models for different types of writing.

Children learn how to write effectively and for a purpose.

Vocabulary, Grammar and Punctuation

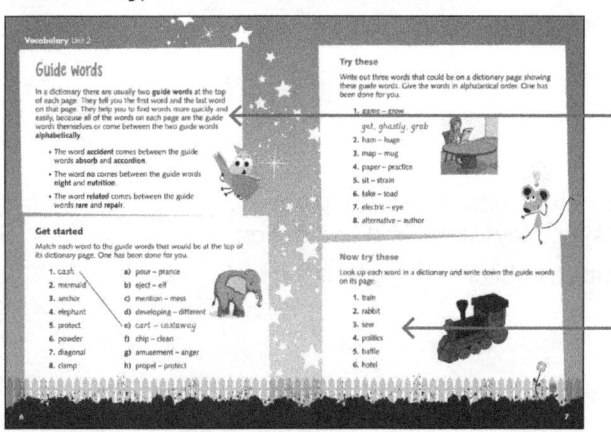

Develops children's knowledge and understanding of grammar and punctuation skills.

A rule is introduced and explained. Children are given lots of opportunities to practise using it.

Spelling

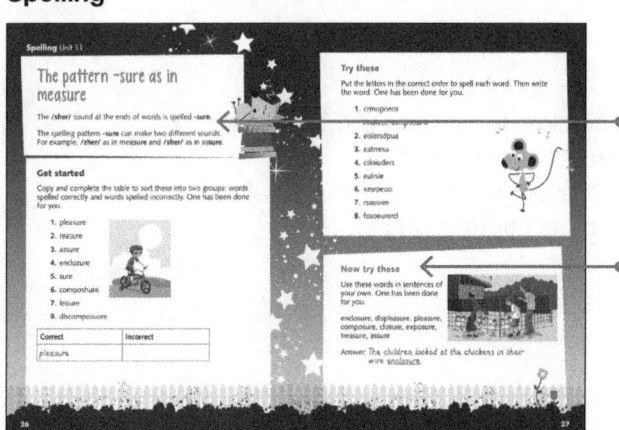

Spelling rules are introduced and explained.

Practice is provided for spotting and using the spelling rules, correcting misspelt words and using the words in context.

About Treasure House

Treasure House on Collins Connect

Digital resources for Treasure House are available on Collins Connect which provides a wealth of interactive activities. Treasure House is organised into six core areas on Collins Connect:

- Comprehension
- Spelling
- Composition
- Vocabulary, Grammar and Punctuation
- The Reading Attic
- Teacher's Guides and Anthologies.

For most units in the Skills Focus Pupil Books, there is an accompanying Collins Connect unit focused on the same teaching objective. These fun, independent activities can be used for initial pupil-led learning, or for further practice using a different learning environment. Either way, with Collins Connect, you have a wealth of questions to help children embed their learning.

Treasure House on Collins Connect is available via subscription at connect.collins.co.uk

Features of Treasure House on Collins Connect

The digital resources enhance children's comprehension, spelling, composition, and vocabulary, grammar, punctuation skills through providing:

- a bank of varied and engaging interactive activities so children can practise their skills independently
- audio support to help children access the texts and activities
- auto-mark functionality so children receive instant feedback and have the opportunity to repeat tasks.

Teachers benefit from useful resources and time-saving tools including:

- teacher-facing materials such as audio and explanations for front-of-class teaching or pupil-led learning
- lesson starter videos for some Composition units
- downloadable teaching notes for all online activities
- downloadable teaching notes for Skills Focus and Integrated English pathways
- the option to assign homework activities to your classes
- class records to monitor progress.

Comprehension

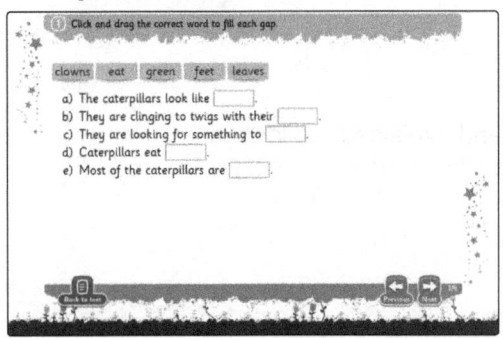

- Includes high-quality text extracts covering poetry, prose, traditional tales, playscripts and non-fiction.
- Audio function supports children to access the text and the activities

Composition

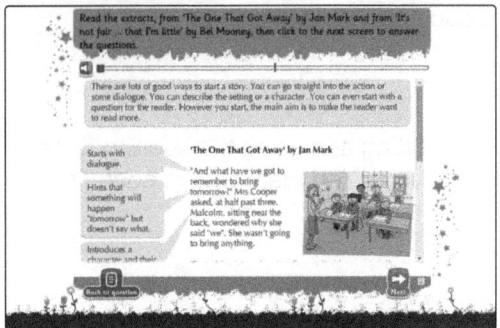

- Activities support children to develop and build more sophisticated sentence structures.
- Every unit ends with a longer piece of writing that can be submitted to the teacher for marking.

About Treasure House

Vocabulary, Grammar and Punctuation

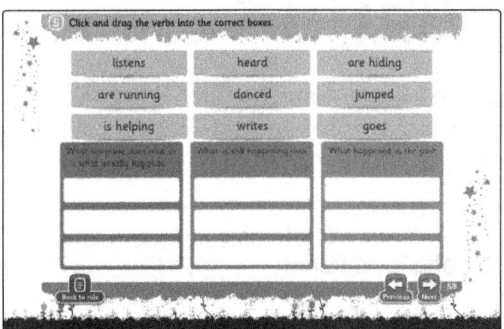

- Fun, practical activities develop children's knowledge and understanding of grammar and punctuation skills.
- Each skill is reinforced with a huge, varied bank of practice questions.

Spelling

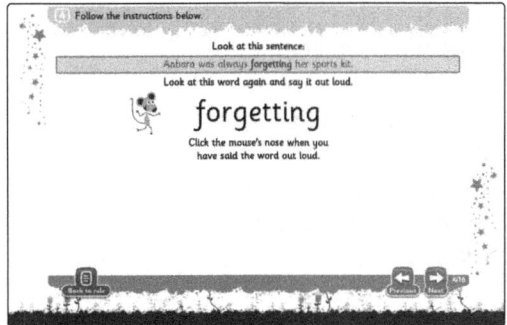

- Fun, practical activities develop children's knowledge and understanding of each spelling rule.
- Each rule is reinforced with a huge, varied bank of practice questions.
- Children spell words using an audio prompt, write their own sentences and practise spelling using Look Say Cover Write Check.

Reading Attic

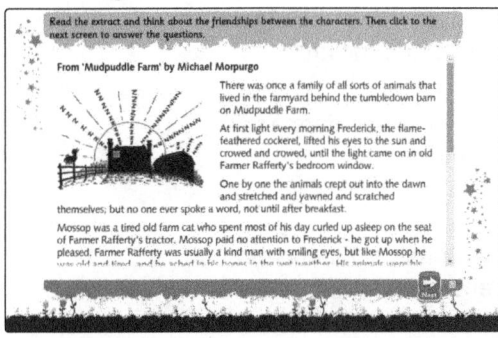

- Children's love of reading is nurtured with texts from exciting children's authors including Michael Bond, David Walliams and Michael Morpurgo.
- Lesson sequences accompany the texts, with drama opportunities and creative strategies for engaging children with key themes, characters and plots.
- Whole-book projects encourage reading for pleasure.

Treasure House Digital Teacher's Guides and Anthologies

The teaching sequences and anthology texts for each year group are included as a flexible bank of resources.

The teaching notes for each skill strand and year group are also included on Collins Connect.

Support, embed and challenge

Treasure House provides comprehensive, detailed differentiation at three levels to ensure that all children are able to access achievement. It is important that children master the basic skills before they go further in their learning. Children may make progress towards the standard at different speeds, with some not reaching it until the very end of the year.

In the Teacher's Guide, Support, Embed and Challenge sections allow teachers to keep the whole class focussed with no child left behind. Two photocopiable resources per unit offer additional material linked to the Support, Embed or Challenge sections.

Support

The Support section offers simpler or more scaffolded activities that will help learners who have not yet grasped specific concepts covered. Background information may also be provided to help children to contextualise learning. This enables children to make progress so that they can keep up with the class.

In Vocabulary, Grammar and Punctuation Teacher's Guides, the activities in the Support section help children to access the rules by giving additional practice of the key teaching point.

If you have a teaching assistant, you may wish to ask him or her to help children work through these activities. You might then ask children who have completed these activities to progress to other more challenging tasks found in the Embed or Challenge sections – or you may decide more practice of the basics is required. Collins Connect can provide further activities.

Embed

The Embed section includes activities to embed learning and is aimed at those who children who are working at the expected standard. It ensures that learners have understood key teaching objectives for the age-group. These activities could be used by the whole class or groups, and most are appropriate for both teacher-led and independent work.

For Vocabulary, Grammar and Punctuation, the activities in Embed enhance children's understanding by offering additional opportunities for the rules to be applied in a variety of contexts.

Challenge

The Challenge section provides additional tasks, questions or activities that will push children who have mastered the concept without difficulty. This keeps children motivated and allows them to gain a greater depth of understanding. You may wish to give these activities to fast finishers to work through independently.

In Vocabulary, Grammar and Punctuation, the challenge activities offer children with the opportunity to work at a higher level by extending the investigation and application of rules to a wider variety of different contexts.

Assessment

Teacher's Guides

There are opportunities for assessment throughout the Treasure House series. The teaching notes in Treasure House Teacher's Guides offer ideas for questions, informal assessment and spelling tests.

Pupil Book Review units

Each Pupil Book has three Review units designed as a quick formative assessment tool for the end of each term. Questions assess the work that has been covered over the previous units. These review units will provide you with an informal way of measuring your pupils' progress. You may wish to use these as Assessment for Learning to help you and your pupils to understand where they are in their learning journey.

The Review units in the Vocabulary, Grammar and Punctuation Pupil Books, include questions testing rules taught in preceding units. By mixing questions on different unit topics within exercises, children can show understanding of multiple rules and patterns.

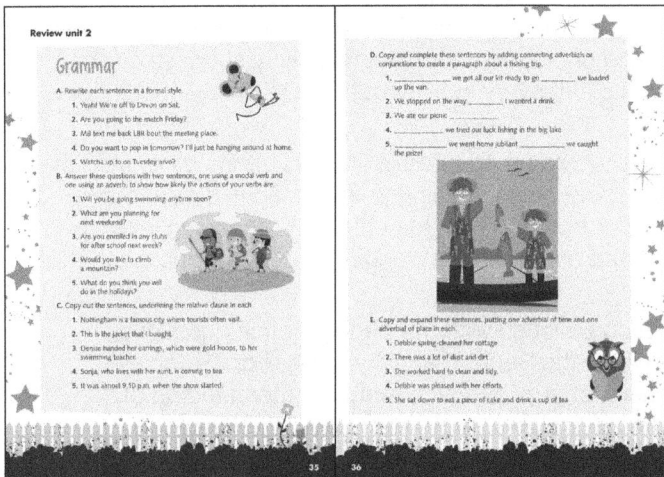

Assessment in Collins Connect

Activities on Collins Connect can also be used for effective assessment. Activities with auto-marking mean that if children answer incorrectly, they can make another attempt helping them to analyse their own work for mistakes. Homework activities can also be assigned to classes through Collins Connect. At the end of activities, children can select a smiley face to indicate how they found the task giving you useful feedback on any gaps in knowledge.

Class records on Collins Connect allow you to get an overview of children's progress with several features. You can choose to view records by unit, pupil or strand. By viewing detailed scores, you can view pupils' scores question by question in a clear table-format to help you establish areas where there might be particular strengths and weaknesses both class-wide and for individuals.

If you wish, you can also set mastery judgements (mastery achieved and exceeded, mastery achieved, mastery not yet achieved) to help see where your children need more help.

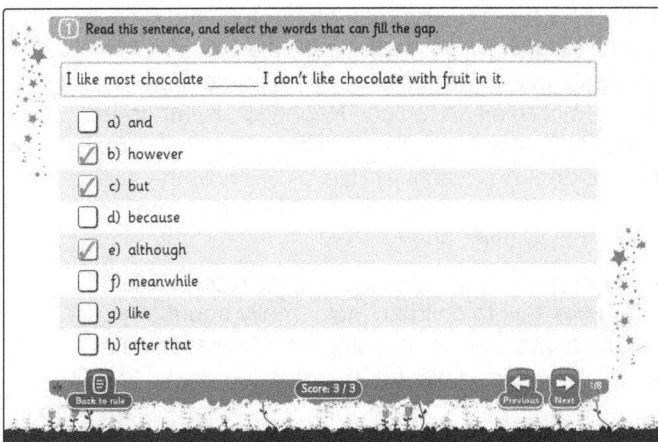

Support with teaching vocabulary, grammar and punctuation

The teacher's guides for Vocabulary, Grammar and Punctuation units can be followed in a simple linear fashion that structures the lesson into four sections:

- assessment of existing skills and knowledge, and an introduction to the unit's teaching point
- completion of the 'pupil practice' questions
- differentiated work, following the Support, Embed and Challenge activity guidance (using the provided photocopiable worksheets)
- homework or additional activities.

However, this lesson structure is intended to be flexible. While we recommend that the first two of these steps should usually be followed in the given order, work following the pupil practice questions can be manipulated in numerous ways to suit the needs, skills and preferences of your class. For example, you may wish to set one of the differentiation activities as homework for the whole class, or to guide children through an 'additional' activity during the lesson, rather than setting it as homework. You may alternatively judge that your class has firmly grasped the concept being taught, and choose not to use any activity suggested, or perhaps introduce only the Extend activity: it is not essential that every activity outlined in the teacher's guide units should be completed.

With the same motivation, many activities (and worksheets) could be adapted for reuse in units other than the one for which they are provided. Several activity and worksheet types are already repeated in similar forms between (and sometimes within) year groups. This is in order both to show the children's changing levels of attainment directly, and to allow any children who have found an activity challenging to reattempt it in a new context after developing their skills.

You may also wish to consider using Support activities in conjunction with the pupil practice questions, if children are struggling with content or a concept with which the Support activity deals. For example, if questions within the 'Try these' and 'Now try these' sections of pupil practice require understanding of adverbials, you may wish to intervene and prepare children using an appropriate Support activity.

By using the teacher's guide units and their suggested activities flexibly, you can choose to tailor the resources at your fingertips to provide the most beneficial learning system for the children being taught. Having confidence in English vocabulary, grammar and punctuation prepares children to function effectively in society as they mature. The aim therefore is to equip children with a strong command of the spoken and written word.

We can make learning vocabulary, grammar and punctuation easy and fun by employing simple techniques to guide children along their literacy journey.

Vocabulary: Establish an ethos in your classroom where words are 'cool'. Talk about your desire to use words that are not the biggest, or the fanciest, or the most complex but that are the 'right words for the job'. Try not to make assumptions about children's level of vocabulary, sometimes those that have a wide vocabulary do not always know the right times to use it. Consider introducing a word of the week, or word of the day. Mention new, unusual or effective words when reading any text in a natural way, for example, say: 'Oh, what a great word I must remember to use that sometime'. Ensure children are so familiar with using dictionaries and thesaurus's that it becomes second nature for them to use them efficiently when reading and writing.

Grammar: Grammar can be tricky to learn and to teach, especially with primary aged children. Explain to them that having a solid working knowledge of grammar enables them to control their spoken and written words in a way that they can influence and affect their reader effectively. Sometimes the very best authors use their knowledge of grammar rules to break them and create interesting effects! Try to make grammar as simple as possible whilst giving enough explanation to be memorable and logical. Repetition is important to help children embed elements of grammar. Another important aspect is demonstrating grammar in real life contexts so children can experience how and why it is needed. A fun activity can be to show the wrong grammar in modeled sentences on the board. This also demonstrates to children how much grammar they have already picked up through their daily use of language, both spoken and written.

Punctuation: Punctuation is generally more straightforward to get to grips with but it does require lots of repetition for children to remember to use it correctly! You can talk to children incidentally about any punctuation marks they come across in wider literature at the same time as focusing on a few aspects at a time through your planned teaching. Model examples of writing with and without punctuation marks to help children notice the different effects.

Delivering the 2014 National Curriculum for English

Unit	Title	Treasure House resources	Collins Connect	English Programme of Study	KS2 English Grammar, Punctuation and Spelling Test code
Vocabulary					
1	Expanded noun phrases	• Vocabulary, Grammar and Punctuation Skills Pupil Book 5, Vocabulary Unit 1, pages 4–5 • Vocabulary, Grammar and Punctuation Skills Teacher's Guide 5 – Vocabulary Unit 1, pages 21–23 – Photocopiable Vocabulary Unit 1, Resource 1: Noun phrase spotter, page 65 – Photocopiable Vocabulary Unit 1, Resource 2: Noun phrase quiz, page 66	Treasure House Vocabulary, Grammar and Punctuation Year 5, Vocabulary Unit 1	Using expanded noun phrases to convey complicated information concisely	G3.2
2	Changing nouns or adjectives into verbs	• Vocabulary, Grammar and Punctuation Skills Pupil Book 5, Vocabulary Unit 2, pages 6–7 • Vocabulary, Grammar and Punctuation Skills Teacher's Guide 5 – Vocabulary Unit 2, pages 24–25 – Photocopiable Vocabulary Unit 2, Resource 1: Verb word search, page 67 – Photocopiable Vocabulary Unit 2, Resource 2: Verb generator, page 68	Treasure House Vocabulary, Grammar and Punctuation Year 5, Vocabulary Unit 2	Converting nouns or adjectives into verbs using suffixes (for example, -ate; -ise; -ify)	G6.3
3A	Verb prefixes (1)	• Vocabulary, Grammar and Punctuation Skills Pupil Book 5, Vocabulary Unit 3A, pages 8–9 • Vocabulary, Grammar and Punctuation Skills Teacher's Guide 5 – Vocabulary Unit 3A, pages 26–27 – Photocopiable Vocabulary Unit 3A, Resource 1: Retake and mistake, page 69 – Photocopiable Vocabulary Unit 3A, Resource 2: Replacing words, page 70	Treasure House Vocabulary, Grammar and Punctuation Year 5, Vocabulary Unit 3	Verb prefixes [for example, dis-, de-, mis-, over- and re-]	G6.2

3B	Verb prefixes (2)	• Vocabulary, Grammar and Punctuation Skills Pupil Book 5, Vocabulary Unit 3B, pages 10–11
		• Vocabulary, Grammar and Punctuation Skills Teacher's Guide 5
		  – Vocabulary Unit 3B, pages 28–29
		  – Photocopiable Vocabulary Unit 3B, Resource 1: Choosing over-, de- or dis-, page 71
		  – Photocopiable Vocabulary Unit 3B, Resource 2: Please disable that toy! page 72
			Treasure House Vocabulary, Grammar and Punctuation Year 5, Vocabulary Unit 3	Verb prefixes [for example, dis-, de-, mis-, over- and re-]	G6.2

Grammar

1	Formal and informal language	• Vocabulary, Grammar and Punctuation Skills Pupil Book 5, Grammar Unit 1, pages 14–15
		• Vocabulary, Grammar and Punctuation Skills Teacher's Guide 5
		  – Grammar Unit 1, pages 31–32
		  – Photocopiable Grammar Unit 1, Resource 1: Formal or informal? page 73
		  – Photocopiable Grammar Unit 1, Resource 2: Watch your language, page 74
			Treasure House Vocabulary, Grammar and Punctuation Year 5, Grammar Unit 1	Recognising vocabulary and structures that are appropriate for formal speech and writing, including subjunctive forms	G7.2
					G7.3
					G7.4

2A	Adverbs showing possibility	• Vocabulary, Grammar and Punctuation Skills Pupil Book 5, Grammar Unit 2A, pages 16–17
		• Vocabulary, Grammar and Punctuation Skills Teacher's Guide 5
		  – Grammar Unit 2A, pages 33–34
		  – Photocopiable Grammar Unit 2A, Resource 1: Definitely maybe, page 75
		  – Photocopiable Grammar Unit 2A, Resource 2: Unquestionably and undoubtedly, page 76
			Treasure House Vocabulary, Grammar and Punctuation Year 5, Grammar Unit 2	Indicating degrees of possibility using adverbs [for example, perhaps, surely]	G1.6

2B	Modal verbs showing possibility	• Vocabulary, Grammar and Punctuation Skills Pupil Book 5, Grammar Unit 2B, pages 18–19
		• Vocabulary, Grammar and Punctuation Skills Teacher's Guide 5
		  – Grammar Unit 2B, pages 35–36
		  – Photocopiable Grammar Unit 2B, Resource 1: We should and we could, page 77
		  – Photocopiable Grammar Unit 2B, Resource 2: I certainly might, page 78
			Treasure House Vocabulary, Grammar and Punctuation Year 5, Grammar Unit 2	Indicating degrees of possibility using modal verbs [for example, might, should, will, must]	G4.1c

3A	Relative clauses (1)	• Vocabulary, Grammar and Punctuation Skills Pupil Book 5, Grammar Unit 3A, pages 20–21
		• Vocabulary, Grammar and Punctuation Skills Teacher's Guide 5
		  – Grammar Unit 3A, pages 37–38
		  – Photocopiable Grammar Unit 3A, Resource 1: Relative clause match, page 79
		  – Photocopiable Grammar Unit 3A, Resource 2: Miss it out? page 80
			Treasure House Vocabulary, Grammar and Punctuation Year 5, Grammar Unit 3	Relative clauses beginning with who, which, where, when, whose, that or an omitted relative pronoun	G3.1a

3B	Relative clauses (2)	• Vocabulary, Grammar and Punctuation Skills Pupil Book 5, Grammar Unit 3B, pages 22–24
		• Vocabulary, Grammar and Punctuation Skills Teacher's Guide 5
		  – Grammar Unit 3B, pages 39–40
		  – Photocopiable Grammar Unit 3B, Resource 1: It's all relative, page 81
		  – Photocopiable Grammar Unit 3B, Resource 2: Add a clause, page 82
			Treasure House Vocabulary, Grammar and Punctuation Year 5, Grammar Unit 3	Relative clauses beginning with who, which, where, when, whose, that or an omitted relative pronoun	G3.1a

4	Linking words in paragraphs	• Vocabulary, Grammar and Punctuation Skills Pupil Book 5, Grammar Unit 4, pages 25–26
		• Vocabulary, Grammar and Punctuation Skills Teacher's Guide 5
		  – Grammar Unit 4, pages 41–42
		  – Photocopiable Grammar Unit 4, Resource 1: Finding connections, page 83
		  – Photocopiable Grammar Unit 4, Resource 2: Making it flow, page 84
			Treasure House Vocabulary, Grammar and Punctuation Year 5, Grammar Unit 4	Devices to build cohesion within a paragraph [for example, then, after, that, this, firstly]	

5A	Adverbials of time	• Vocabulary, Grammar and Punctuation Skills Pupil Book 5, Grammar Unit 5A, pages 27–28
		• Vocabulary, Grammar and Punctuation Skills Teacher's Guide 5
		  – Grammar Unit 5A, pages 43–44
		  – Photocopiable Grammar Unit 5A, Resource 1: Last month at the farm, page 85
		  – Photocopiable Grammar Unit 5A, Resource 2: When did that happen? page 86
			Treasure House Vocabulary, Grammar and Punctuation Year 5, Grammar Unit 5	Linking ideas across paragraphs using adverbials of time [for example, later], place [for example, nearby], and number [for example, secondly] or tense choices [for example, he had seen her before]	G1.6a
					G4.2

5B	Adverbials of place	• Vocabulary, Grammar and Punctuation Skills Pupil Book 5, Grammar Unit 5B, pages 29–30
		• Vocabulary, Grammar and Punctuation Skills Teacher's Guide 5
		  – Grammar Unit 5B, pages 45–46
		  – Photocopiable Grammar Unit 5B, Resource 1: Over the hill and far away, page 87
		  – Photocopiable Grammar Unit 5B, Resource 2: Where did he go? page 88
			Treasure House Vocabulary, Grammar and Punctuation Year 5, Grammar Unit 5	Linking ideas across paragraphs using adverbials of time [for example, later], place [for example, nearby], and number [for example, secondly] or tense choices [for example, he had seen her before]	G1.6a
					G4.2

5C	Adverbials of manner	• Vocabulary, Grammar and Punctuation Skills Pupil Book 5, Grammar Unit 5C, pages 31–32
		• Vocabulary, Grammar and Punctuation Skills Teacher's Guide 5
		  – Grammar Unit 5C, pages 47–48
		  – Photocopiable Grammar Unit 5C, Resource 1: Sentences with style, page 89
		  – Photocopiable Grammar Unit 5C, Resource 2: How did she do that? page 90
			Treasure House Vocabulary, Grammar and Punctuation Year 5, Grammar Unit 5	Linking ideas across paragraphs using adverbials of time [for example, later], place [for example, nearby], and number [for example, secondly] or tense choices [for example, he had seen her before]	G1.6a
					G4.2

5D	Adverbials of number	• Vocabulary, Grammar and Punctuation Skills Pupil Book 5, Grammar Unit 5D, pages 33–34
		• Vocabulary, Grammar and Punctuation Skills Teacher's Guide 5
		  – Grammar Unit 5D, pages 49–50
		  – Photocopiable Grammar Unit 5D, Resource 1: Adverbials of number game, page 91
		  – Photocopiable Grammar Unit 5D, Resource 2: How often? page 92
			Treasure House Vocabulary, Grammar and Punctuation Year 5, Grammar Unit 5	Linking ideas across paragraphs using adverbials of time [for example, later], place [for example, nearby], and number [for example, secondly] or tense choices [for example, he had seen her before]	G1.6a
					G4.2

Punctuation				

1	Using commas for clearer meaning	• Vocabulary, Grammar and Punctuation Skills Pupil Book 5, Punctuation Unit 1, pages 37–38
		• Vocabulary, Grammar and Punctuation Skills Teacher's Guide 5
		  – Punctuation Unit 1, pages 52–53
		  – Photocopiable Punctuation Unit 1, Resource 1: Comma quiz, page 93
		  – Photocopiable Punctuation Unit 1, Resource 2: Commas galore, page 94
			Treasure House Vocabulary, Grammar and Punctuation Year 5, Punctuation Unit 1	Use of commas to clarify meaning or avoid ambiguity in writing	G5.6a

2	Hyphens	• Vocabulary, Grammar and Punctuation Skills Pupil Book 5, Punctuation Unit 2, pages 39–40
		• Vocabulary, Grammar and Punctuation Skills Teacher's Guide 5
		  – Punctuation Unit 2, pages 54–55
		  – Photocopiable Punctuation Unit 2, Resource 1: Compound adjective generator, page 95
		  – Photocopiable Punctuation Unit 2, Resource 2: The super-useful hyphen, page 96
			Treasure House Vocabulary, Grammar and Punctuation Year 5, Punctuation Unit 2	How hyphens can be used to avoid ambiguity [for example, man eating shark versus man-eating shark, or recover versus re-cover]	G5.13

3	Brackets, dashes and commas	• Vocabulary, Grammar and Punctuation Skills Pupil Book 5, Punctuation Unit 3, pages 41–42
		• Vocabulary, Grammar and Punctuation Skills Teacher's Guide 5
		  – Punctuation Unit 3, pages 56–57
		  – Photocopiable Punctuation Unit 3, Resource 1: Parenthesis practice, page 97
		  – Photocopiable Punctuation Unit 3, Resource 2: Commas, brackets and dashes, page 98
			Treasure House Vocabulary, Grammar and Punctuation Year 5, Punctuation Unit 3	Using brackets, dashes or commas to indicate parenthesis	G5.9

4	Boundaries between clauses	• Vocabulary, Grammar and Punctuation Skills Pupil Book 4, Punctuation Unit 5, pages 43–44
		• Vocabulary, Grammar and Punctuation Skills Teacher's Guide 5
		  – Punctuation Unit 4, pages 58–59
		  – Photocopiable Punctuation Unit 4, Resource 1: Colon – semicolon – dash, page 99
		  – Photocopiable Punctuation Unit 4, Resource 2: After the dash, page 100
			Treasure House Vocabulary, Grammar and Punctuation Year 5, Punctuation Unit 4	Using the semi-colon, colon and dash to mark the boundary between independent clauses [for example, It's raining; I'm fed up]	G5.10
					G5.11
					G5.12

5	Colons to introduce lists	• Vocabulary, Grammar and Punctuation Skills Pupil Book 5, Punctuation Unit 5, pages 45–46
		• Vocabulary, Grammar and Punctuation Skills Teacher's Guide 5
		  – Punctuation Unit 5, pages 60–61
		  – Photocopiable Punctuation Unit 5, Resource 1: I love: cakes, tea and more cakes, page 101
		  – Photocopiable Punctuation Unit 5, Resource 2: Roll the dice, page 102
			Treasure House Vocabulary, Grammar and Punctuation Year 5, Punctuation Unit 5	Use of the colon to introduce a list	G5.10

6	Punctuating bulleted lists	• Vocabulary, Grammar and Punctuation Skills Pupil Book 5, Punctuation Unit 6, pages 47–48
		• Vocabulary, Grammar and Punctuation Skills Teacher's Guide 5
		  – Punctuation Unit 6, pages 62–63
		  – Photocopiable Punctuation Unit 6, Resource 1: Bullet it, page 103
		  – Photocopiable Punctuation Unit 6, Resource 2: Bullet list poster, page 104
			Treasure House Vocabulary, Grammar and Punctuation Year 5, Punctuation Unit 6	Punctuation of bullet points to list information consistently	G5.14

Vocabulary Unit 1: Expanded noun phrases

Overview

English curriculum objectives
- Using expanded noun phrases to convey complicated information concisely

Treasure House resources
- Vocabulary, Grammar and Punctuation Skills Pupil Book 5, Vocabulary Unit 1, pages 4–5
- Collins Connect Treasure House Vocabulary, Grammar and Punctuation Year 5 Vocabulary, Unit 1
- Photocopiable Vocabulary Unit 1, Resource 1: Noun phrase spotter, page 65
- Photocopiable Vocabulary Unit 1, Resource 2: Noun phrase quiz, page 66

Introduction

Teaching overview

A noun phrase can be as simple as a determiner and a noun (the castle), or can include further detail provided by adjectives (the distant, gloomy castle) or a prepositional phrase (the distant, gloomy castle on the bend in the river). The activities in the Pupil Book provide practice first in adding adjectives, then adding prepositional phrases. Children should be familiar with noun phrases from Year 4; this unit provides practice in creating more expansive phrases.

Introduce the concept

Ask the children if any of them can tell you what a noun phrase is. Elicit suggestions and establish that a noun phrase is a phrase that works as a noun and provides more information about the noun. Write the word 'dog' on the board. Agree that this is a noun. Add 'the' to create 'the dog'. Ask: 'Is this a noun or a noun phrase?' Agree that it is a noun phrase – the simplest type. Now add 'hairy, brown' between 'the' and 'dog'. Ask: 'What have I added here?' Agree that two different adjectives have been used. Ask: 'What other information can we use?' Add 'with muddy paws' and ask what this is (a prepositional phrase). Ask volunteers to come to the front and add the labels 'noun', 'determiner', 'adjective', 'adjective' and 'prepositional phrase'.

Write the word 'cat' on the board and ask the children to work in their tables to create a noun phrase (including a determiner, at least two adjectives and a prepositional phrase), write it on a mini whiteboard and hold it up. Ask the children to read all the other phrases and decide which table's phrase is the best.

Pupil practice

Pupil Book pages 4–5

Get started

Children copy and expand the noun phrases, focusing on adding two suitable adjectives before the nouns.

Answers

Open-ended questions: accept any two appropriate adjectives per noun phrase, punctuated correctly. [1 mark per question] For example:

1. *the green, scale snake* [example]
2. a dark, windy storm
3. my comfortable, thick mattress
4. the red, shiny apple
5. a tall, thin child
6. that green, wooden table
7. Sorrell's heavy, winter coat
8. our white, fluffy poodle
9. Liam's heavy, leather bag
10. one bright, sunny morning

Try these

Read the sentences together, locating the noun phrase in each. Ask: 'What do these phrases comprise?' Agree that each is a determiner, two adjectives and a noun. Ask the children in pairs to locate and name each element. Ask them to write out the sentences as they stand, then expand them by adding a prepositional phrase to further enhance the noun phrase.

Answers

Accept any appropriate prepositional phrase [1 mark per question]. For example:

1. *among the leaves.* [example]
2. that she wore last year.
3. that was only a week old.
4. beneath an old apple tree.
5. in the park.
6. that drowned out the noise of the television.
7. near his new house.
8. with a torn cover.

Vocabulary Unit 1: Expanded noun phrases

Now try these

Ask the children to expand each noun with adjectives and a prepositional phrase, and then use it in a sentence. Ask the children to discuss and improve their sentences by sharing them with a partner before writing them down.

Answers

Accept any appropriate sentences that expand the noun with adjectives and a prepositional phrase. [1 mark per question] For example:

1. I walked into the deep, dark cave at the foot of the cliff.
2. She could see a large, makeshift treehouse with a flag hanging over the edge.
3. Joshua jumped on his shiny, new motorbike with a 600 cc engine.
4. Mindy wanted to borrow a book from the quiet, dark library at the top of the tower.
5. Naman rode the little, grey pony with a long mane.
6. I need a dark red, loose costume covered with beads to wear for the play.
7. Manoj wrote a short, happy story about animals.

Support, embed & challenge

Support

Cut out the words and phrases from the chart on Vocabulary Unit 1 Resource 1: Noun phrase spotter. Ask the children to help you sort them into three piles: adjectives, noun phrases and prepositional phrases. Start by locating the adjectives, then the noun phrase. Once the words are sorted, pick up one of the noun phrases and ask: 'What do I need to do to this phrase to make it into a noun?' (remove the determiner). Cut up the noun phrases, spread out all the words and phrases and work together to create expanded noun phrases, first adding the adjectives then the prepositional phrases. Look at the phrases together then challenge the children to take turns to change one of the words, or the whole prepositional phrase, to slowly change each noun phrase to something completely different. Provide the children with individual copies of the resource sheet and ask them to complete it independently.

Answers

	Noun phrase	Adjective	Prepositional phrase
stone		/	
in the paper bag			/
a bag	/		
with the dusty cover			/
the horse	/		
with silver buckles			/
on top of the hill			/
the book	/		
golden		/	
ancient		/	
his sweets	/		
leather		/	
with the long mane			/
chewy		/	
a castle	/		

Embed

Organise the children into pairs and provide each pair with the words and phrases from Vocabulary Unit 1 Resource 1: Noun phrase spotter in a bag or hat. Ask them to take turns to take a slip of paper out of the bag and say whether it is an adjective, a noun phrase or a prepositional phrase before using it to create their own noun phrase. Provide the children with individual copies of Vocabulary Unit 1 Resource 2: Noun phrase quiz to revise and consolidate the content from the unit.

Vocabulary Unit 1: Expanded noun phrases

(**Answers** 1. A noun is a word that names people, places or things; 2. For example, a cat, a book, a purse; 3. Noun phrase = all options; 4. An adjective is a word that describes a noun.; 5. For example, green, happy, old; 6. Open-ended question; 7. A prepositional phrase tells you where or when something happened.; 8. For example, in the paper bag.; 9. Open-ended question; 10. Open-ended question)

Challenge
Challenge the children to choose six interesting sentences from a book they have been reading. Ask them to write them in large writing on a sheet of paper. Ask them to look for the nouns, adjectives, noun phrases and prepositional phrases. Tell them to use coloured pens to label the different parts of the sentence.

Homework / Additional activities

Ask the children to write four different expanded noun phrases for the noun 'house'. Challenge them to create a completely different atmosphere with each phrase, for example 'the smart, luxury penthouse brimming with mod cons', 'the crumbling remains of an old croft house just visible through the bracken'.

Collins Connect: Vocabulary Unit 1
Ask the children to complete Vocabulary Unit 1 (see Teach → Year 5 → Vocabulary, Grammar and Punctuation → Vocabulary Unit 1).

Vocabulary Unit 2: Changing nouns or adjectives into verbs

Overview

English curriculum objectives
- Converting nouns or adjectives into verbs using suffixes (for example: '–ate', '–ise' and '–ify')

Treasure House resources
- Vocabulary, Grammar and Punctuation Skills Pupil Book 5, Vocabulary Unit 2, pages 6–7
- Collins Connect Treasure House Vocabulary, Grammar and Punctuation Year 5, Vocabulary Unit 2
- Photocopiable Vocabulary Unit 2, Resource 1: Verb word search, page 67
- Photocopiable Vocabulary Unit 2, Resource 2: Verb generator, page 68

Introduction

Teaching overview
Nouns and adjectives can be turned into verbs using the suffixes '–ate', '–en', '–ise' and '–ify', for example: 'originate', 'lengthen', 'standardise' and 'solidify'. Sometimes the noun or adjective will need to have an existing suffix removed before the suffix is used to create the verb, for example: 'communication' → 'communicate', 'critical' → 'criticise', 'apology' → 'apologise', 'horror' → 'horrify', 'intense' → 'intensify', 'beauty' → 'beautify'.

Introduce the concept
Recap on suffixes and explain to the children that some nouns and adjectives can be turned into verbs using the suffixes '–ate', '–en', '–ise' and '–ify'. Write the following on the board and discuss how the words have changed:

- straight (adjective) + –en (suffix) = straighten (verb)
- elastic (adjective and noun) + –ate = elasticate (verb)
- advert (noun) + –ise (suffix) = advertise (verb)
- sign (noun) + –ify (suffix) = signify (verb)

Explain that different verbs take different suffixes, so we have 'strengthen' not 'strengthate', 'advertise' not 'advertify', and the children need to learn which word is the correct one. Write the four suffixes on the board and ask the children, working in groups, to add one suffix to each of: 'comment', 'solid', 'fright' and 'modern'. Share the words and their word classes.

Point out that we sometimes have to remove an existing ending before adding the new one. Write the following pairs of words on the board and ask the children to locate which letters have been removed from the original word, which suffix has been added and how the word class has changed: accessory → accessorise; animation → animate; terror → terrify.

Pupil practice
Pupil Book pages 6–7

Get started
Children look at the two columns of words and match the verbs to the noun or adjective they come from. Once the children have written their pairs of words, ask them to attribute a word class to each word, underline the suffix in each verb, and underline any suffix that has been removed from the original noun or adjective.

1. dramatise – d) drama [example]
2. purify – a) pure [1 mark]
3. horrify – f) horror [1 mark]
4. ripen – c) ripe [1 mark]
5. categorise – e) category [1 mark]
6. strengthen – b) strength [1 mark]

Try these
Ask the children to copy and complete the sentences by changing the underlined word into the correct verb, using a suffix from the box. The first answer has been completed as an example.

Example answers
1. The shops will <u>advertise</u> the January sale shortly. [example]
2. The strawberry mousse will <u>solidify</u> in the fridge. [1 mark]
3. We have been working very hard to understand when we should and should not <u>hyphenate</u> words with prefixes. [1 mark]
4. My dad loves to play tricks and <u>frighten</u> me! [1 mark]
5. Our teacher wanted to <u>standardise</u> the way we presented our homework. [1 mark]
6. Cleaning your teeth every day will help keep them healthy and also <u>brighten</u> them. [1 mark]
7. The children needed to <u>classify</u> their project work under different topic headings. [1 mark]
8. The whole school was planning to <u>decorate</u> the hall for the summer concert. [1 mark]

Vocabulary Unit 2: Changing nouns or adjectives into verbs

9. Can we confirm and <u>finalise</u> our plans concerning getting to the bus stop for the school trip? [1 mark]
10. The soldiers worked hard throughout the night to <u>fortify</u> the king's castle. [1 mark]

Now try these

Children change each word into a verb and then use it in a sentence. Ask them to discuss what the verbs will be and share ideas for their sentences before writing them. Pause once the children have established what the verbs are to discuss the spelling of 'flatten'.

Answers

Accept any appropriate sentence that includes the correct verb: 'magnify', 'apologise', 'lessen', 'activate', 'animate', 'flatten', 'simplify', 'minimise'.

[1 mark per correct word and 1 mark per appropriate sentence.]

Support, embed & challenge

Support

Fill in a copy of Vocabulary Unit 2 Resource 2: Verb generator and cut out the words. Together pair up the words and discuss word class, spelling and meaning.

Ask the children to use Vocabulary Unit 2 Resource 1: Verb word search to help them become more familiar and more confident with vocabulary ending in the suffixes '–ate', '–en', '–ise' and '–ify'. Once they've completed the word search ask them to cut out the two word lists and match up and investigate the pairs of words.

Answers

a	u	t	h	o	r	i	s	e	d	c
s	d	k	y	l	n	g	g	w	k	o
s	a	c	f	o	f	a	l	e	q	m
a	r	t	l	o	d	j	o	h	f	p
s	k	m	r	s	b	v	r	m	r	u
s	e	o	i	e	l	m	i	e	i	t
i	n	t	e	n	s	i	f	y	g	e
n	h	i	u	i	z	f	y	a	h	r
a	d	v	e	r	t	i	s	e	t	i
t	c	a	p	t	i	v	a	t	e	s
e	a	t	o	n	c	j	b	p	n	e
g	s	e	x	f	a	l	s	i	f	y

Embed

Provide the children with copies of Vocabulary Unit 2 Resource 2: Verb generator and ask them to create a verb from each noun or adjective. Afterwards, ask them to take three of the pairs of words they have created and write a sentence for each of the six words, in order to illustrate how the words have changed.

(**Answers** whiten, illustrate, brighten, realise, maximise, intensify, operate, justify, beautify, investigate, deafen, specialise, loosen, emphasise, estimate, notify, motivate, deepen, apologise, solidify, straighten, terrorise, calculate, symbolise)

Challenge

Challenge the children to go on a suffix hunt. Ask them to scan through the pages of a book they are currently reading and write down any words that use the suffixes '–ify', '–ise', '–en or '–ate'. Ask them to think about which nouns or adjectives they come from. Then ask them to make a poster to display their results.

Homework / Additional activities

Ask children to find five further word examples of nouns or adjectives turned into verbs by having the suffix '–ify', '–ise', '–en' or '–ate' added to them.

Collins Connect: Vocabulary Unit 2

Ask the children to complete Vocabulary Unit 2 (see Teach → Year 5 → Vocabulary, Grammar and Punctuation → Vocabulary Unit 2).

Vocabulary Unit 3A: Verb prefixes (1)

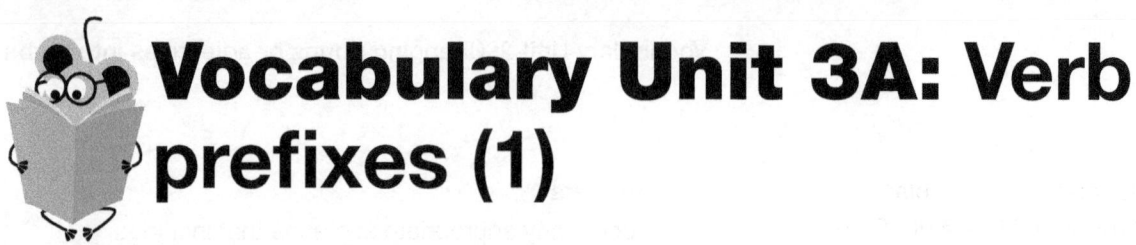

Overview

English curriculum objectives
- Verb prefixes (for example: 'dis–', 'de–', 'mis–', 'over–' and 're–')

Treasure House resources
- Vocabulary, Grammar and Punctuation Skills Pupil Book 5, Vocabulary Unit 3A, pages 8–9
- Collins Connect Treasure House Vocabulary, Grammar and Punctuation Year 5, Vocabulary Unit 3

- Photocopiable Vocabulary Unit 3A, Resource 1: Retake and mistake, page 69
- Photocopiable Vocabulary Unit 3A, Resource 2: Replacing words, page 70

Additional resources
- The following words on separate slips of paper: giving, shape, laid, understood, deed, guided, heard, judged, placed, book, act, apply, deliver, join, fit, tell, think, take, move, name, read, view, visit, wind

Introduction

Teaching overview
This unit covers the prefixes 'mis–' and 're–', both of which the children will have encountered in their Year 3 and 4 spelling programmes. Here the focus is on word class and meaning. Added to the beginning of a word, 'mis–' means 'badly' or 'incorrectly', and changes the verb into a negative version of itself, for example: 'misbehave' and 'mistake'. The prefix 're–' means 'again' or sometimes 'back', for example: 'return', 'restate' and 'reclaim'.

Introduce the concept
Ask the children if they can remember what a prefix is. Elicit suggestions and establish that a prefix is a group of letters that can be added to the beginning of a word to change its meaning. Explain that the focus today will be adding 'mis–' and 're–' to words to create verbs with new meanings.

- misbehave = behave badly ('mis–' means 'badly' or 'incorrectly')
- reappear = appear again ('re–' means 'again' or 'back')

Give each group of children a few of the word slips (see Additional resources above) and ask them to add 'mis–' or 're–' to each word, writing the new words on a whiteboard. Explain that most words will only take one or the other prefix, but they might find that some of their words will work with both prefixes, for example 'retake' and 'mistake'. Ask a volunteer from each group to bring their whiteboard to the front of the class and share the words they have created and what they mean (using the meaning of the prefix as part of their definition if possible).

Pupil practice

Pupil Book pages 8–9

Get started
Remind the children of the meaning of the prefixes 'mis–' and 're–', and ask them to use this knowledge to write a definition and then a sentence for each word. Remind the children that each word is a verb.

Answers
1. *To rebuild means to build again.* [example]
2. To rewrite means to write again. [1 mark]
3. To replace means to place back. [1 mark]
4. To reopen means to open again. [1 mark]
5. To repay means to pay back. [1 mark]
6. To misdirect means to direct incorrectly. [1 mark]
7. To mislead means to lead incorrectly. [1 mark]
8. To mismatch means to match up incorrectly. [1 mark]
9. To misjudge means to judge incorrectly. [1 mark]
10. To misuse means to use badly. [1 mark]

Accept any sentences that use the word correctly. [1 mark per sentence]

Try these
Ask the children to copy and complete the sentences, adding a prefix from the box to the word in brackets. The first answer has been completed as an example.

Answers
1. *Your dinner has gone cold now, but I can reheat it for you in a few minutes.* [example]
2. I think he misheard me because he arrived at the wrong time. [1 mark]
3. Lucas was asked to rewrite some homework that he had done badly. [1 mark]

Vocabulary Unit 3A: Verb prefixes (1)

4. Mr Melchett <u>reentered</u> the study because he'd left his glasses in there. [1 mark]
5. I was very embarrassed because I <u>mistook</u> him for the mayor. [1 mark]
6. Because they misjudged the traffic, Tabitha and Sabine missed the beginning of the show. [1 mark]
7. I have <u>reconsidered</u> and I am going to let you go to Emma's house after all. [1 mark]
8. My father realised that he had <u>misplaced</u> the boarding cards as we arrived at the gate. [1 mark]

Now try these
Ask the children to add the same prefix ('re–' or 'mis–') to all the words in each set and then use them all in a short paragraph. You may wish to support children by discussing the task before setting them to work independently or in pairs.

Answers
1. Accept any appropriate short paragraph that includes 'misinform', 'misplace' and 'misunderstand'. [3 marks]
2. Accept any appropriate short paragraph includes 'redirect', 'reapply' and 'reactivate'. [3 marks]
3. Accept any appropriate short paragraph that includes 'misspell', 'misconstrue' and 'miscommunicate'. [3 marks]
4. Accept any appropriate short paragraph that includes 'replay', 'retake' and 'refit'. [3 marks]

Support, embed & challenge

Support
Reuse the slips from the starter, giving a set of words to pairs of children. Ask them to discuss which words can take which prefix and sort them into piles: those that take 're–', those that take 'mis–' and those that can take both. Share the words that the pairs found. Provide the children with Vocabulary Unit 3A Resource 1: Retake and mistake and ask them to carry out the activity, trying both prefixes with each word before writing the new word in one or both of the columns. Encourage the children to use a dictionary to look up the words. Some words may be placed in both column, for example: 'take'. Note: there are some nouns and adjectives as well as verbs.

(**Answers** Re–: build, heat, write, entered, use, take, place, open, pay, direct, estimate, appear, considered, fit, apply, activate, play; Mis–: advise, use, take, place, judge, direct, estimate, behave, heard, fortune, fit, inform, understand, spell, construe, communicate, treat)

Embed
Ask the children to carry out Vocabulary Unit 3A Resource 2: Replacing words. This will provide practice in using words that begin with the prefixes 're–' and 'mis–' in sentences.

When they have finished, ask the children to work out which words from the box could have the prefix replaced ('mis–' for 're–', or 're–' for 'mis–'). Challenge them to find the three words and write a sentence for each one.

(**Answers** 1. replace; 2. misdirect; 3. repay; 4. misjudged; 5. misadvise; 6. rebuild; 7. misuse; 8. rewrite)

Challenge
Challenge the children to find as many words as they can that begin with the prefixes 're–' and 'mis–' and create these as a long list for display. Then ask them to choose four words from their list that are new to them and present the words plus their meanings to a group or the class.

Homework / Additional activities
Ask children to go on a prefix hunt. Ask them to scan through the pages of a book they are currently reading and write down words that use the prefixes 're–' or 'mis–'. Ask if they can tell which root words form them. Collect all the words the children have found to create a poster to display their results.

Collins Connect: Vocabulary Unit 3
Ask the children to complete Vocabulary Unit 3 (see Teach → Year 5 → Vocabulary, Grammar and Punctuation → Vocabulary Unit 3).

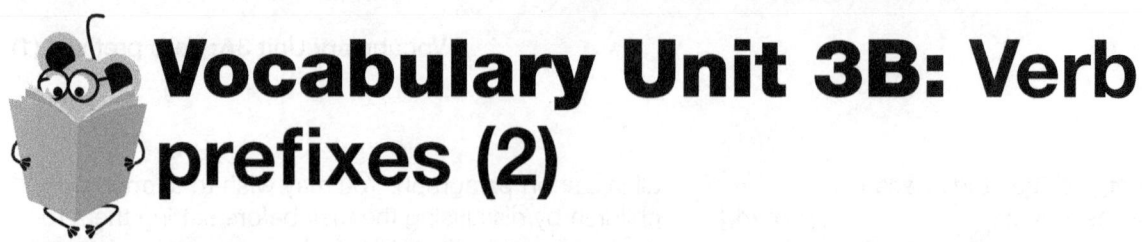
Vocabulary Unit 3B: Verb prefixes (2)

Overview

English curriculum objectives
- Verb prefixes (for example: 'dis–', 'de–', 'mis–', 'over–' and 're–')

Treasure House resources
- Vocabulary, Grammar and Punctuation Skills Pupil Book 5, Vocabulary Unit 3B, pages 10–11
- Collins Connect Treasure House Vocabulary, Grammar and Punctuation Year 5, Vocabulary Unit 3B

- Photocopiable Vocabulary Unit 3B, Resource 1: Choosing over–, de– or dis–, page 71
- Photocopiable Vocabulary Unit 3B, Resource 2: Please disable that toy! page 72

Additional resources
- Word cards: compensate, react, crowded, loaded, value, ice, mist, stress, compose, clutter, forest, advantage, agree, honest, obedient, please, continue, trust, infect, arm

Introduction

Teaching overview
This unit covers the prefixes 'de–' (meaning 'remove', or 'take away'), 'dis–' (makes the opposite) and 'over–' (meaning 'too much'). The children should learn to use their knowledge of prefixes to understand new words.

Introduce the concept
Ask the children to remind you and each other of the definition of a prefix, remembering the prefixes covered in the last unit. Ask why we might need to know about adding prefixes to words. Remind the children that a prefix is a group of letters that can be added to the beginning of a word to change its meaning. Show the following examples on the board:

- overload = too much of something ('over–' means 'excessive' or 'too much')
- disobey = fail to obey ('dis–' means 'not' or 'opposite of')
- demist = to remove the mist from a window ('de–' means 'remove')

Remind the children that each prefix can only go with certain words. Hand out a few word cards (see Additional resources) to each group and ask the children to work together to add 'over–', 'dis–' or 'de–' to each one. Create three columns on the board, headed 'over–', 'dis–' and 'de–', and ask volunteers to come to the front and write one of the words they've created in their group in the appropriate column.

Pupil practice

Pupil Book pages 10–11

Get started
Recap on the meaning of each of the three prefixes: 'over–', 'dis–' and 'de–'. Encourage the children to use this knowledge to create their definition. Tell the children to look up any words they do not know, but only after predicting what they think the word means. They then put the word in a sentence.

Answers
Accept any appropriate sentence that includes a form of the word in the Pupil Book.
[2 marks for each question.]

Try these
Ask the children to copy and complete the sentences, adding a prefix from the box to go with the word in brackets. The first answer has been completed as an example.

Answers

1. My friend Suki and her brother Jay <u>disagreed</u> quite seriously yesterday morning. [example]
2. Leon missed last week's dress rehearsal, which really <u>displeased</u> our director. [1 mark]
3. We had to hold sports day when the weather was boiling, so we drank lots of water to make sure we didn't <u>dehydrate</u> in the heat. [1 mark]
4. I really am trying hard not to <u>overreact</u> to what you just said, but I'm so cross! [1 mark]
5. It was very difficult walking through town today – the sales are really <u>overcrowding</u> the streets. [1 mark]
6. Dad <u>overpaid</u> on his tax account so he is due to get a refund. [1 mark]

28

Vocabulary Unit 3B: Verb prefixes (2)

7. I tried to call Auntie Sarah in Australia but the call <u>disconnected</u>. [1 mark]

8. We had to <u>decipher</u> the secret code before we could read what the message said. [1 mark]

Now try these
Explain to the children that they can only use one of the prefixes for each set of words – creating three words that start the same. Encourage them to create their sentences verbally, trying out different options, before they write. Tell them to ensure that they understand the meaning of each new word, checking in a dictionary if necessary.

Answers
Accept any appropriate short paragraph that includes the correct words:

1. distrust, dishonour and disapprove. [3 marks]
2. overfill, overeat and overcook. [3 marks]
3. debone, defrost and decode. [3 marks]
4. disconnect, disintegrate and discount. [3 marks]

Support, embed & challenge

Support
Complete your own copy of Vocabulary Unit 3B Resource 1: Choosing over–, de– or dis– and cut out the words you have created. Work with the children in a group and display the words in the middle of the table. Take each word in turn and read it with the children, asking them to tell you what it means, encouraging them to use the meaning of the prefix in their definition. Ask them to take a word each and locate the prefix in the word and then cut it away. Ask them to tell the rest of the group what their remaining (root) word means, then add the prefix and say what it means now. Muddle up all the roots and prefixes and work together to match them up to recreate all the words you started with.

Ask the children to carry out Vocabulary Unit 3B Resource 1: Choosing over–, de– or dis–. Encourage the children to use a dictionary to look up the words (selecting a dictionary that includes most of these words) where needed. Note: there are a few common nouns and adjectives as well as verbs. (**Answers** Over–: load, fill, qualify, value, estimate, statement, eat, cook, react, crowding, paid; De–: code, activate, rail, value, forest, congest, scribe, fuse, hydrate, bone, frost, cipher; Dis– able, honour, appoint, approve, obey, qualify, connect, agreed, integrate, count, pleased, order, trust)

Embed
Ask the children to use Vocabulary Unit 3B Resource 2: Please disable that toy! to practice adding and using words with these prefixes. Tell them to first add the prefixes to the words in the box and then to use the words to complete the sentences. Note: there are some nouns as well as verbs here. (**Answers** 1. deice; 2. overestimate; 3. decode; 4. overfilled; 5. disable; 6. disappoint; 7. derail; 8. deforestation)

Challenge
Challenge the children to find as many words as they can that begin with the prefixes 'de–', 'dis–' and 'over–'. Then ask them to choose four words from their list that are new to them and present the words plus their meanings to a group or the class.

Homework / Additional activities

Ask children to go on a prefix hunt. Ask them to scan through the pages of a book they are currently reading and write down words that use the prefixes 'de–', 'dis–' and 'over–'. Ask if they can tell which root words form them. Tell them to make a poster to display their results.

Collins Connect: Vocabulary Unit 3
Ask the children to complete Vocabulary Unit 3 (see Teach → Year 5 → Vocabulary, Grammar and Punctuation → Vocabulary Unit 3).

Review unit 1: Vocabulary

Pupil Book pages 12–13

A. Ask children to add two appropriate subjectives before each noun.

Example answers

1. the <u>moist, spongy</u> cake [1 mark]
2. a <u>squawking, colourful</u> bird [1 mark]
3. that <u>old, blue</u> bicycle [1 mark]
4. the <u>exciting, new</u> movie [1 mark]
5. Laura's <u>expensive, black</u> piano [1 mark]

B. Ensure that the children have expanded the nouns (rather than just extended the sentence) and that the whole phrase can be read as a noun unit. Ask children to add two appropriate subjectives before each noun.

Example answers

1. starring her favourite actor. [1 mark]
2. hidden behind his shoes. [1 mark]
3. with the bubbling spring water. [1 mark]
4. of the Eiffel Tower. [1 mark]
5. full of bubbles. [1 mark]

C. Ask children to remove the suffixes and write the root word.

Answers

1. advert [1 mark]
2. solid [1 mark]
3. hyphen [1 mark]
4. fright [1 mark]
5. standard [1 mark]

D. Ask children to copy and complete the sentences with the word in brackets and an appropriate suffix.

Answers

1. My cousin has a tendency to <u>dramatise</u> every event in her life. [1 mark]
2. The vet advised us to <u>medicate</u> our poorly hamster. [1 mark]
3. I knew that our new tree house would <u>horrify</u> the neighbours. [1 mark]
4. The label on the packet of plums said '<u>ripen</u> at home'. [1 mark]
5. Some people say you can <u>strengthen</u> your bones and teeth by drinking milk. [1 mark]

E. Ask children to copy and complete the sentences with the word in brackets and an appropriate suffix.

Answers

1. I had to <u>rebuild</u> my sandcastle after the dog knocked it down. [1 mark]
2. Very slowly our old car overtook the great big lorry broken down on the hill. [1 mark]
3. I'm convinced I made at least three <u>mistakes</u> in my literacy work. [1 mark]
4. The puppy is so cute – but he is very <u>disobedient</u>. [1 mark]
5. Patti's sudden hiccup made everyone laugh and <u>defused</u> Mum's anger. [1 mark]

Grammar Unit 1: Formal and informal language

Overview

English curriculum objectives
- Recognising vocabulary and structures that are appropriate for formal speech and writing, including subjunctive forms

Treasure House resources
- Vocabulary, Grammar and Punctuation Skills Pupil Book 5, Grammar Unit 1, pages 14–15
- Collins Connect Treasure House Vocabulary, Grammar and Punctuation Year 5, Grammar Unit 1
- Photocopiable Grammar Unit 1, Resource 1: Formal or informal? page 73
- Photocopiable Grammar Unit 1, Resource 2: Watch your language, page 74

Introduction

Teaching overview

This unit builds on children's knowledge and understanding of formal and informal language. Here, the activities build on choosing quite straightforward differences between formal and informal language. As the children develop their spoken and written skills they will be able to focus their speech and language appropriately on the spectrum between informal and formal language. Ensure that the children are clear on the difference between the terms 'formal' and 'informal' and the terms 'Standard' and 'non-Standard English' as they are related but not interchangeable. It is also important that the children understand that informal English is not wrong – it is just sometimes inappropriate. When modelling the teaching point, use your voice to show emphasis, intonation, tone, volume and natural speech patterns. This will help children to learn the differences between spoken and written vocabulary, grammar and punctuation.

Introduce the concept

Explain to the children that we use formal language to speak to people that we do not know and to write letters. We use informal language to talk to friends and to write emails and texts. Write the following example lists of features on the board to demonstrate – or ask the children what they think the features of formal and informal language are and elicit the ideas in these lists:

- Informal: contractions, incomplete sentences, words missed out, shorter words and slang; can be Standard or non-Standard English
- Formal: no contractions, only complete sentences, careful word choices, polite and respectful language; always Standard English.

Ask a volunteer to come to the front and ask them to demonstrate how they would ask a friend if they would like a sweet (for example: 'Want one?'). Next ask them to say how they would ask the Queen if she would like a cup of tea (for example: 'Excuse me Ma'am, but would you care for a cup of tea?'). Explain that there is not one type of informal language nor one type of formal language, but we must judge in each situation how formal or informal it is appropriate to be.

Pupil practice
Pupil Book pages 14–15

Get started

After they have completed the activity, ask the children to articulate what made each sentence 'formal' or 'informal'. Challenge the children to create a (verbal) formal version of the informal sentences.

Answers
1. *informal* [example]
2. formal [1 mark]
3. informal [1 mark]
4. formal [1 mark]
5. formal [1 mark]
6. informal [1 mark]
7. informal [1 mark]
8. formal [1 mark]

Try these

Ask the children to copy out the more informal sentence from each pair. The first answer has been completed as an example.

Answers
1. *Watching that rocket launch on TV tonight?* [example]
2. Don't worry 'bout what she said. [1 mark]

Grammar Unit 1: Formal and informal language

3. Lots to tell yer! [1 mark]
4. Let me know ASAP. [1 mark]
5. What? [1 mark]
6. D'ya have your mobile? [1 mark]

Now try these

Ask the children to rewrite each sentence in a formal style by changing the underlined words. Encourage the children to read the original and their revised versions out loud. Precise wording will vary.

Suggested answers
1. What <u>do you</u> think <u>about</u> that new film? [2 marks]
2. Did you say <u>you had</u> seen something good on <u>television</u>? [2 marks]
3. <u>I am</u> not <u>doing</u> anything wrong. [2 marks]
4. <u>They are</u> saying <u>you had</u> seen it. [2 marks]
5. Is it <u>all right</u> for our plans that <u>it is supposed</u> to be raining on Saturday? [3 marks]
6. I know <u>you are</u> just joking, but <u>you had</u> better calm down <u>as soon as possible</u>! [3 marks]

Support, embed & challenge

Support

Together, role-play situations that involve informal and more formal language, such as finding a phone in the park and asking friends and then a stranger if it is their phone; or playing football with friends then asking for their ball back from a neighbour. Discuss the difference between Standard and non-Standard English, then move on to discuss formal language. Carry out the activity in 'Embed' as a piece of shared writing.

Cut out the squares from Grammar Unit 1, Resource 1: Formal or informal?, put them in a bag and ask the children to take turns to pull out a phrase and read it to the group using a formal or informal voice as appropriate (correcting any misapprehension that this means putting on a posh voice or losing their accent). Identify less-formal ways that language can be presented in speech or with familiar recipients. Provide the children with individual copies of the resource sheet and ask them to colour in the squares as indicated. (**Answers** Examples of informal language: That's so cool,; What you up to?; Just hanging around.; Don't you hate it when that happens?; What about Tuesday?; Mmm, not sure.; I am so looking forward to seeing this show.; Had a good time?; Ahh, so cute!; I dunno.; Sounds like a good plan)

Embed

Ask the children to look at Grammar Unit 1, Resource 2: Watch your language to encourage them to translate informal examples of language into a formal style. Ask children to read and discuss the sentences provided then rewrite them in a formal style.

(**Possible answers** 1. I thought I would stop and say hello.; 2. The garden is a terrible mess.; 3. There are a lot of things we could do.; 4. I must leave.; 5. Let us sort it out later.; 6. What are you doing tomorrow?; 7. Let us see what the others are doing.; 8. These party invitations are great. Do you agree?)

Then ask the children, working in pairs, to write two invitations: the first a note to a friend asking them to a party, the second to invite the local member of parliament to attend a school concert.

Challenge

Challenge the children to find examples of formal and informal language in texts in the classroom and online. Ask them to present examples as a poster and label the features.

Homework / Additional activities

Ask children to a) find an advert that uses informal language (reminding them that it might still be written in Standard English but might use slang words and a chatty style) and b) ask family members for a letter that they have received that uses formal language. Share the examples that the children have found.

Collins Connect: Grammar Unit 1

Ask the children to complete Grammar Unit 1 (see Teach → Year 5 → Vocabulary, Grammar and Punctuation → Grammar Unit 1).

Grammar Unit 2A: Adverbs showing possibility

Overview

English curriculum objectives
- Indicating degrees of possibility using adverbs (for example: 'perhaps' and 'surely')

Treasure House resources
- Vocabulary, Grammar and Punctuation Skills Pupil Book 5, Grammar Unit 2A, pages 16–17
- Collins Connect Treasure House Vocabulary, Grammar and Punctuation Year 5, Grammar Unit 2
- Photocopiable Grammar Unit 2A, Resource 1: Definitely maybe, page 75
- Photocopiable Grammar Unit 2A, Resource 2: Unquestionably and undoubtedly, page 76

Introduction

Teaching overview
This unit revises the word class of adverbs but develops children's awareness of the way adverbs can be used to show possibility. The children should be encouraged to use a wide range of these adverbs of possibility to show nuances in both their spoken and written work.

Introduce the concept
Ask the children if they can recall and explain the definition of an adverb. Elicit that adverbs can describe or give more information about a verb, or how a verb is performed. Explain to the children that adverbs can also show how likely the action of a verb is – these adverbs are called adverbs of possibility. Write the following examples on the board to demonstrate:

- Adverbs: perhaps, maybe, possibly, definitely, certainly, surely, rarely, occasionally, unquestionably, absolutely, undoubtedly, generally, usually

Write the sentence: 'I am the funniest person in the class' on the board. Ask different volunteers to come to the front and add one of the adverbs from the list to the sentence, for example, 'I am rarely the funniest person in the class' or 'I am unquestionably the funniest person in the class'. Discuss the nuances between similar words, deciding which is better.

Pupil practice

Pupil Book pages 16–17

Get started
Ask the children to copy out the sentences, underlining the adverb of possibility in each one. The first answer has been completed as an example. You may wish to support the children by reading each sentence aloud, then pausing while they find and point to the adverb of possibility, before asking them to copy the sentences.

1. "<u>Surely</u> there's something fun we can do this weekend," I said to Dad. [example]
2. Dad looked at the weather forecast and finally made a suggestion: <u>possibly</u> sailing! [1 mark]
3. "<u>Definitely</u>," Mum replied with a big grin. [1 mark]
4. I <u>certainly</u> wanted to go – I've loved our sailing holidays ever since I was a little boy. [1 mark]
5. Dad said he could <u>probably</u> borrow his friend's sailing boat. [1 mark]
6. "<u>Perhaps</u> we could invite Grandpa, too?" I asked Dad. [1 mark]
7. He replied that we <u>absolutely</u> should. [1 mark]
8. "Grandpa is <u>generally</u> a great help," he added. [1 mark]

Try these
Ask the children to copy out the sentence from each pair that seems most likely to happen. The first answer has been completed as an example.

Answers
1. *I'll probably go home.* [example]
2. We usually go sailing. [1 mark]
3. I unquestionably enjoy swimming. [1 mark]
4. You'll definitely win. [1 mark]
5. It will undoubtedly be sunny. [1 mark]
6. We will certainly have a barbecue. [1 mark]

Now try these
Ask the children to answer each question with a sentence using an adverb of possibility. You may wish to support children by discussing the task before setting them to work independently or in pairs.

Grammar Unit 2A: Adverbs showing possibility

Possible answers

Accept any appropriate sentences that contain an adverb of possibility.

1. The weather will definitely be nice at the weekend. [1 mark]
2. I am possibly going on holiday this year. [1 mark]
3. Tomorrow evening I am certainly going to my friend's house for dinner. [1 mark]
4. After school I usually go straight home. [1 mark]
5. Yes, I would unquestionably like to learn to scuba dive. [1 mark]
6. Perhaps for my birthday I will have a party. [1 mark]

Support, embed & challenge

Support

Ask the children to use Grammar Unit 2A, Resource 1: Definitely maybe to become more familiar and confident with a wider range of adverbs of possibility. Ask children to locate and circle the adverbs of possibility in the word search. Then use four of the words they have found in the sentences at the bottom.

Cut out the words from Grammar Unit 2A, Resource 2: Unquestionably and undoubtedly and put them in a hat. Work with these children in a group: they take turns to take a word from the hat, read it and create a sentence that uses the words – with support and ideas from the rest of the group. Provide simple sentences to use as a starting point if the children need further support, for example: 'I usually win.' 'I am very sensible.' 'I make spelling mistakes.' 'I am organised.'

Answers

o	c	c	a	s	i	o	n	a	l	l	y
e	q	e	m	h	y	p	a	f	h	y	d
p	e	r	h	a	p	s	b	o	c	x	e
o	n	t	f	l	u	u	s	g	u	i	f
s	m	a	y	b	e	r	q	k	w	t	i
s	a	i	k	s	m	e	v	d	u	k	n
i	j	n	n	p	z	l	e	j	s	r	i
b	o	l	a	w	l	y	l	j	u	a	t
l	i	y	u	b	d	z	d	g	a	r	e
y	y	i	t	r	w	z	g	x	l	e	l
f	v	e	g	e	n	e	r	a	l	l	y
h	s	c	o	r	p	t	x	q	y	y	r

Embed

Ask the children to work in pairs and give each pair a copy of Grammar Unit 2A, Resource 2: Unquestionably and undoubtedly and a dice and ask them to carry out the activity. After a few minutes, when the children are confidently creating sentences, challenge them to change each other's sentences, changing the adverb as the dice dictates.

Challenge

Challenge to children to write a story about a family who are considering emigrating to live in a different country. Tell them to use lots of adverbs in the story to show the likelihood of them moving.

Homework / Additional activities

Challenge children to find as many examples of adverbs of possibility as they can in their current reading book.

Collins Connect: Grammar Unit 2

Ask the children to complete Grammar Unit 2 (see Teach → Year 5 → Vocabulary, Grammar and Punctuation → Grammar Unit 2).

The Connect activity provides further practice in recognising and choosing both adverbs of possibility and modal verbs. You might choose to use this resource once the children have completed Grammar Unit 2B below.

Grammar Unit 2B: Modal verbs showing possibility

Overview

English curriculum objectives
- Indicating degrees of possibility using modal verbs (for example: 'might', 'should', 'will' and 'must')

Treasure House resources
- Vocabulary, Grammar and Punctuation Skills Pupil Book 5, Grammar Unit 2B, pages 18–19
- Collins Connect Treasure House Vocabulary, Grammar and Punctuation Year 5, Grammar Unit 2
- Photocopiable Grammar Unit 2B, Resource 1: We should and we could, page 77
- Photocopiable Grammar Unit 2B, Resource 2: I certainly might, page 78

Introduction

Teaching overview

This unit introduces the concept of modal verbs used to show how likely something is. The children should be encouraged to use modal verbs to add nuances in both their spoken and written work. The modal verbs 'can', 'could', 'would', 'shall', 'may', 'might', 'should', 'must' and 'will' change the verb.

Introduce the concept

Tell the children that in this lesson they will learn about and practice using modal verbs. Ask if any of them have heard of modal verbs before, and if they have, ask them to share their prior knowledge with the class. Explain that modal verbs are used to show how likely something is. Draw a comparison with adverbs of possibility and explain that sometimes an adverb of possibility is used alongside a modal verb.

Write the following examples of modal verbs on the board: 'can', 'could', 'may', 'might', 'must', 'ought', 'shall', 'should', 'will' and 'would'. Write the sentence: 'I eat my broccoli' on the board. Add the modal verb 'will' to give, 'I will eat my broccoli.' Ask other volunteers to change the choice of modal verbs to change the meaning of the sentences.

If the children are confident with this, challenge them to now add an adverb of possibility, for example:' I definitely should eat my broccoli.'

Ask the children to work in their groups to add a different modal verb to each of the following: 'We go for a walk.' 'I look after my brother.' 'Caitlin does her homework.' 'Leon tidies his room.' (In the last two examples the existing verb will need to change.)

Pupil practice

Pupil Book pages 18–19

Get started

Ask the children to copy out the sentences, underlining the modal verb in each one. The first answer has been completed as an example. You may wish to support the children by reading each sentence aloud, then pausing while they find and point to the modal verb, before asking them to copy the sentences.

Answers

1. "<u>Could</u> we go fishing on Saturday?" I asked Dad. [example]
2. "We <u>should</u> be able to," he replied. [1 mark]
3. I told him I <u>would</u> get my fishing kit packed and ready. [1 mark]
4. "I <u>will</u> prepare you a tasty picnic," said Mum with a wink. [1 mark]
5. "<u>Shall</u> we invite Uncle Tony?" Dad asked me. [1 mark]
6. "You <u>ought</u> to," piped up Mum. "He always invites you two." [1 mark]
7. "He <u>might</u> be busy on Saturday," I said. "He goes to the match most weeks." [1 mark]
8. "I <u>can</u> ask him later tonight," said Dad. [1 mark]

Try these

Ask the children to copy out the sentence from each pair that seems most likely. The first answer has been completed as an example.

Answers

1. We will follow her. [example]
2. I should help. [1 mark]
3. I can come with you into town. [1 mark]
4. I shall go to the shops with Gran and help her carry her bags. [1 mark]
5. I must finish my homework. [1 mark]
6. I will walk the dog. [1 mark]

35

Grammar Unit 2B: Modal verbs showing possibility

Now try these

Ask the children to answer each question with a sentence using a modal verb to show how likely the action is. You may wish to support children by discussing the task before setting them to work independently or in pairs.

Possible answers

Accept any appropriate sentences that contain a modal verb.

1. The weather could be nice tomorrow. [1 mark]

2. Open-ended question: I should be going to the cinema on Saturday. [1 mark]

3. Open-ended question: Next Tuesday I may go to the library. [1 mark]

4. Open-ended question: After school I am not going to the library because I ought to go to my friend's house. [1 mark]

5. Open-ended question: Yes, I would like to learn to abseil. [1 mark]

6. Open-ended question: At the weekend I think I might go to the park. [1 mark]

Support, embed & challenge

Support

Ask the children to complete Grammar Unit 2B Resource 1: We should and we could to practice using modal verbs. Once the children have finished, ask the children to compare their answers with a partner. In each instance where they have chosen a different word, ask them to decide whose sentence is more likely to happen. Next ask them to try out each word in the box in each sentence and decide together whether they fit or not. (**Answers** 1. could; 2. must; 3. should; 4. may; 5. will; 6. would; 7. can; 8. might)

Embed

Ask the children to work in pairs. Tell the children to write the words 'can', 'could', 'may', 'might', 'must', 'ought', 'shall', 'should', 'will' and 'would' on a small whiteboard. Tell them to take turns to choose a word from the list and make up an oral sentence. Tell them to award one point for making up a sentence, two points if the sentence contains two modal verbs and three points if the sentence builds on the last sentence their partner said.

When the children are confidently using modal verbs, ask them to use Grammar Unit 2B Resource 2: I certainly might to practice combining them with adverbs of possibility to create more complicated sentences. Ask children to answer each question by using one modal verb and one adverb of possibility. Explain that they can combine verbs and adverbs, for example: 'She said she definitely will come.' Or they might want to use them in different clauses, for example: 'She might not be able to, but she is definitely going to try.' The words in the boxes can be use multiple times.

Challenge

Challenge the children to write a story about a group of children on an activity day. Tell them to include a range of modal verbs and adverbs of possibility in the story to show the likelihood of them participating in a variety of new activities such as canoeing and abseiling.

Homework / Additional activities

Challenge children to find as many examples of modal verbs of possibility as they can in their current reading book. Ask them to write out five of these sentences, changing the modal verb to give a different meaning to the sentence.

Collins Connect: Grammar Unit 2

Ask the children to complete Grammar Unit 2 (see Teach → Year 5 → Vocabulary, Grammar and Punctuation → Grammar Unit 2).

Grammar Unit 3A: Relative clauses (1)

Overview

English curriculum objectives
- Relative clauses beginning with 'who', 'which', 'where', 'when', 'whose', 'that' or an omitted relative pronoun

Treasure House resources
- Vocabulary, Grammar and Punctuation Skills Pupil Book 5, Grammar Unit 3A, pages 20–21
- Collins Connect Treasure House Vocabulary, Grammar and Punctuation Year 5, Grammar Unit 3
- Photocopiable Grammar Unit 3A, Resource 1: Relative clause match, page 79
- Photocopiable Grammar Unit 3A, Resource 2: Miss it out? page 80

Introduction

Teaching overview
This unit introduces children to the concept of using relative clauses and relative pronouns to give more information about nouns. A relative clause is a subordinate clause that is introduced by a relative pronoun 'which', 'who', 'that', 'whose' or a relative adverb 'where' or 'when'. In some situations, the relative pronoun can be omitted, for example: 'Do you have the book (that) I lent you?'

Introduce the concept
You may wish to introduce the concept by eliciting any prior knowledge the children have of relative clauses and pronouns, but if you suspect that for most children in the class this is a new area, you may prefer to proceed with explaining the concept to them directly. Explain that we use relative clauses to give more information about nouns. We can start a relative clause with a relative pronoun: 'who', 'that', 'which' or 'whose' or a relative adverb 'where' or 'when'.

For example:
- There's my neighbour who won the sprint at school.
- Look at my house, which has a red door and a brass letterbox.

Point out the relative clause and the noun it gives further information about.

Write the words 'who', 'that', 'which', 'whose', 'where' and 'when' on the board and ask the children to work in their groups to write a sentence using one of them. Remind them that this sentence won't be a question and the relative clause will give further information about the noun that is the subject of the sentence. Share the sentences the groups have created, remodelling them where necessary and writing them on the board. Look out for any using 'which' and 'that' where the relative pronoun could be omitted, for example: 'Trisha gave me back the jumper (that) I'd left at her house.' 'There's the girl (whom) I was telling you about.'

Pupil practice

Pupil Book pages 20–21

Get started
Ask the children to copy the sentences, underlining the relative clause in each. You may wish to support the children by reading each sentence aloud, then pausing while they find and point to the relative clause, before asking them to copy the sentences. Afterwards, ask the children to turn to their neighbour and say what noun the relative clause refers to.

Answers
1. *Priya, who comes with me to football training, is my neighbour.* [example]
2. Today is our annual sports day, which is always exciting.
3. Faye is an amazing athlete who always gives her best.
4. This is the game that I want to buy with my pocket money.
5. Today is the day when I start my new reading programme.
6. I will be walking over the mountain where the explorer went!
7. I have a new pencil case that has a secret compartment.
8. My cousin is the girl whose jumper is covered in bright red polka dots.

Try these
Ask the children to complete the sentences with an appropriate relative pronoun or relative adverb. When they have finished, ask: 'Which sentences did not need a relative pronoun? What could we have used?'

37

Grammar Unit 3A: Relative clauses (1)

Answers
1. Devon is a seaside county <u>where</u> people often go on holiday.
2. These are the trainers <u>(that/which)</u> I bought.
3. Pratik, <u>whom</u> I sit next to, has been helping me.
4. Look at these photos <u>(that/which)</u> I took of Millie.
5. I have a friend <u>who</u> is an amazing singer.
6. Salma handed her glasses, <u>which/that</u> were broken, to her PE teacher.
7. Damara's art partner was Marek, <u>whose</u> paintings were always the best.
8. It was almost 8:30 a.m. <u>when</u> Nat finally arrived.

Now try these
Ask the children to copy and complete the sentences by finishing the relative clause. You may wish to support children by discussing their sentences before setting them to work independently.

Answers
Open-ended questions: accept any relative clause appropriate to the relative pronoun.

[1 mark per question]

Support, embed & challenge

Support
Work with the children in a group. Cut out the sentence halves from Grammar Unit 3A Resource 1: Relative clause match and place them in the middle of the group. First work together to sort the sentence halves into main and relative clauses. Then ask the children to help you pair up the two halves. Ask the children to tell you what noun the relative clause describes. Provide the children with individual copies of the resource sheet and ask them to create the sentences and stick them in their book. Return to the original slips and remove the relative clauses. Ask the children to choose a sentence starter and suggest a new relative clause to complete the sentence.
(**Answers** Sandra is my riding instructor who only talks about horses.; I have a new plan which involves working extra hard.; Football practice finishes at seven o'clock when it starts to get dark.; This is the skateboard that I have been saving up to buy.; Today is the last day of term which means a lie-in tomorrow.; Look at these messages that are from my mum.; My uncle is the man whose hair is slicked over to one side.; I love winter mornings when there is frost all over the grass.; This is the swimming pool where Mum brings us on Saturday mornings.; I went down the road that leads to the supermarket.; Lewis is an excellent golfer whose successes are always in the news.; Paris is the city where you can see the Eiffel Tower.)

Embed
Provide the children with the following sentences: 'That's the boy I met yesterday.' and 'Tidy the mess you made in your bedroom!' Explain that both of them have a relative pronoun that is omitted (but understood by the reader). Challenge them to work out which pronoun is missing ('that'/'who' and 'that'). Provide the children with individual copies of Grammar Unit 3A Resource 2: Miss it out? to enable the children to experiment with the effect of removing relative pronouns in sentences.

(**Answers** 1. whom – yes, it would work without.; 2. who – no; 3. that – yes; 4. where – no; 5. that – yes; 6. that – no; 7. when – no; 8. that – yes; 9. where – no; 10. that – yes)

Challenge them to write two sentences of their own that use relative clauses with an omitted relative pronoun.

Challenge
Challenge children to choose and copy out six sentences that contain examples of relative clauses. Ensure they have underlined and labelled the main part of each sentence, as well as identifying the relative clause.

Provide these children with copies of Grammar Unit 3A Resource 1: Relative clause match and ask them to first match up the sentences then decide if they would prefer to embed the relative clause in the middle of the main clause to make a more elegant sentence.

Homework / Additional activities
Ask children to write a list of all the relative pronouns they can find in their reading book.

Collins Connect: Grammar Unit 3
Ask the children to complete Grammar Unit 3 (see Teach → Year 5 → Vocabulary, Grammar and Punctuation → Grammar Unit 3).

You might choose to use this resource once the children have completed Grammar Unit 3B below.

Grammar Unit 3B: Relative clauses (2)

Overview

English curriculum objectives
- Relative clauses beginning with 'who', 'which', 'where', 'when', 'whose', 'that' or an omitted relative pronoun

Treasure House resources
- Vocabulary, Grammar and Punctuation Skills Pupil Book 5, Grammar Unit 3B, pages 22–24
- Collins Connect Treasure House Vocabulary, Grammar and Punctuation Year 5, Grammar Unit 3
- Photocopiable Grammar Unit 3A, Resource 2: Miss it out?, page 80
- Photocopiable Grammar Unit 3B, Resource 1: It's all relative page 81
- Photocopiable Grammar Unit 3B, Resource 2: Add a clause, page 82

Introduction

Teaching overview
This unit builds on Grammar Unit 3A. The relative clause can either be essential information: 'That's the girl who helped me' (a defining clause); or extra information: 'Tara, who is wearing the red jumper, helped me yesterday' (a non-defining clause). A relative clause that is a non-defining clause is usually separated out using commas, or brackets. A defining relative clause does not need commas.

Introduce the concept
Recap on relative clauses, asking each group to give you a sentence with a relative clause. Explain that sometimes the information in the relative clause is essential, for example: 'Michael Morpurgo is the author whom we are studying this term'. And sometimes the relative clause is additional non-essential information, for example: 'Michael Morpurgo, whom we are studying this term, wrote *Kensuke's Kingdom*.' Point out that we could remove the relative clause here and would be left with 'Michael Morpurgo wrote *Kensuke's Kingdom*.' Explain that when a relative clause is extra non-essential information, we put it in commas, or even brackets. Ask the children to work in their groups to punctuate – or not:

Penny who wanted a turn started crying immediately.

The Friary Leisure Centre which is next to the school is our closest swimming pool.

Sophie gave me a sweet when I fell over.

Mrs Barker is the teacher I like the best.

Ask: 'Where is the relative pronoun in the last sentence?' Agree that it would be 'who' but it has been omitted.

Pupil practice

Pupil Book pages 22–24

Get started
Ask the children to first locate the relative clause then decide if it is essential or extra information. If they are unsure, suggest that they try removing the clause and read the rest of the sentence – if it makes sense then the relative clause is extra information.

Answers
1. I'll practise my guitar at six o'clock, <u>when my favourite programme is over</u>. extra [example]
2. essential [1 mark]
3. extra [1 mark]
4. extra [1 mark]
5. extra [1 mark]
6. essential [1 mark]
7. essential [1 mark]
8. essential (though with commas it would be extra information but the sentence would have a slightly different focus) [1 mark]

Try these
Answers
1. Devon, where we're going camping, is a five-hour drive away. [example]
2. It was almost 8:30 a.m. when the alarm went off. [1 mark]
3. My book, which Jasmine's reading as well, is brilliant. [1 mark]
4. There is a new grocer's shop in town where you can buy great pineapples. [1 mark]
5. The puppy, which was only five weeks old, chewed my school books. [1 mark]
6. I'm going to the stables, where I feel at my happiest, to calm down. [1 mark]

39

Grammar Unit 3B: Relative clauses (2)

7. We always have our Music lesson at 4 p.m. when everyone else is going home. [1 mark]
8. We are going on holiday to Iceland where it is very cold. [1 mark]

Now try these

Ask the children to try out different options verbally with a partner before writing down their completed sentences. Ask them to check to see if commas are necessary.

Answers

Accept any appropriate and well-punctuated sentences. [2 marks per sentence]

Support, embed & challenge

Support

Cut out the sentences from Grammar Unit 3A Resource 2: Miss it out? and ask the children to choose a sentence and work with a partner to underline the relative clause. Ask the children if anyone has a sentence with a relative clause in the middle of it. Read the sentence and then help each pair to write a new sentence placing the relative clause from the original sentence in the middle of the new sentence, for example: 'The lady, whom I told you about, is just crossing the road.' 'The shop, where Mum once left her purse, has closed down.'

Carry out Grammar Unit 3B Resource 1: It's all relative as a shared task, asking the children to first locate the noun that is going to be described further. Discuss the back story to this noun and then ask them to help you create the sentence. Look at the sentences together and decide in which sentences the relative clause is essential.

Embed

Use Grammar Unit 3B Resource 1: It's all relative to enable children to experiment and practice writing their own relative clauses that are suitable to complete the sentences provided. Ask children to read and complete the sentences by adding their own relative clauses.

Afterwards, ask them to leave their completed sheets on their desk and go around the room reading each other's ideas. Provide the children with a new version of the sheet and ask them to complete the sentences with new ideas, if possible using different relative pronouns or adverbs.

Challenge

Ask the children to complete Grammar Unit 3B, Resource 2: Add a clause. Encourage them to first locate the noun at the beginning of the sentence and then create a clause to supply additional information about it.

Challenge these children to discover the difference between 'which' and 'that', and experiment with different sentences. (Technically, 'which' introduces a non-defining clause, for example: 'The hat, which I like, is red', meaning 'The hat is red'; 'that' introduces a defining clause, for example: 'The hat that I like is red', meaning, in other words 'I like the red hat'.)

Homework / Additional activities

Ask children to write three sentences that use relative clauses.

Collins Connect: Grammar Unit 3

Ask the children to complete Grammar Unit 3 (see Teach → Year 5 → Vocabulary, Grammar and Punctuation → Grammar Unit 3).

Grammar Unit 4: Linking words in paragraphs

Overview

English curriculum objectives
- Devices to build cohesion within a paragraph (for example: 'then', 'after', 'that', 'this' and 'firstly')

Treasure House resources
- Vocabulary, Grammar and Punctuation Skills Pupil Book 5, Grammar Unit 4, pages 25–26
- Collins Connect Treasure House Vocabulary, Grammar and Punctuation Year 5, Grammar Unit 4
- Photocopiable Grammar Unit 4, Resource 1: Finding connections, page 83
- Photocopiable Grammar Unit 4, Resource 2: Making it flow, page 84

Introduction

Teaching overview
This unit introduces children to the concept that paragraphs are used to make a long piece of writing easier to read and we can use special words to help the reader understand the connections between the ideas in a piece of writing. We can use a range of conjunctions such as 'but', 'so' and 'because', or adverbs and adverbial phrases such as 'luckily', 'As soon as I'd arrived' and 'after that'. Reading any of their writing aloud will help children to hear where further linking words would be helpful.

Introduce the concept
Explain to the children that paragraphs make a long piece of writing easier to read. Confirm that a paragraph is a group of sentences about one idea or topic. Tell the children that we often use special words to help the reader understand the connections between ideas in a piece of writing. We can use linking words and phrases to help the reader see these connections between sentences and clauses in a paragraph. Show the following examples on the board to demonstrate:

Phrases:
- First of all …
- After that …
- Finally …

Linking words:
- … so …
- … but …
- … because …

Pupil practice

Pupil Book pages 25–26

Get started
Ask the children to copy out the sentences, underlining the linking words and phrases. You may wish to support the children by reading the sentences aloud, then pausing while they think about and point at the linking words and phrases before asking them to write the sentences. The first answer has been completed as an example.

Answers
1. <u>In the beginning</u>, the swimming pool was open every day. [example]
2. It was popular, <u>but</u> it needed money for repairs. [1 mark]
3. <u>After that</u>, it could not afford to open more than three days a week. [1 mark]
4. <u>Now</u>, unless we raise more money, the swimming pool will be demolished. [1 mark]
5. We will, <u>as a result</u>, not have anywhere to go swimming. [1 mark]
6. <u>Next</u>, we will try a new plan: we will hold a charity street party. [1 mark]
7. <u>Finally</u>, people have noticed our efforts and they have bought hundreds of tickets. [1 mark]
8. <u>Because of this</u>, the council has offered to double our money. [1 mark]

Try these
Ask the children to copy and complete the sentences by adding connecting adverbials or conjunctions to create a paragraph about a day out. The first answer has been completed as an example. The connectives chosen will vary.

Possible answers
1. <u>First of all</u>, we went on the swings <u>and then</u> we went on the seesaw. [example]
2. We had a great time <u>that morning</u>. [1 mark]
3. We stopped <u>because</u> I wanted a drink. [1 mark]
4. We stopped for lunch <u>a little bit later</u>. [1 mark]

41

Grammar Unit 4: Linking words in paragraphs

5. <u>Afterwards</u>, we walked around the forest. [1 mark]
6. <u>It was then that we realised</u> it was cold. [1 mark]
7. We got back to the bus stop <u>after another hour</u>. [1 mark]
8. <u>Finally</u>, we went home <u>as</u> I was shattered. [2 marks]

Now try these

Ask the children to use linking words and phrases to write the stated paragraphs. You may wish to support children by discussing their ideas before setting them to work independently.

Possible answers

1. Accept any short paragraph about a new species of insect that uses linking words and phrases. [5 marks max]
2. Accept any short paragraph about a new theme-park ride that uses linking words and phrases. [5 marks max]
3. Accept any short paragraph about a club or sport the children enjoy that uses linking words and phrases. [5 marks max]
4. Accept any short paragraph about making some food that uses linking words and phrases. [5 marks max]
5. Accept any short paragraph about what the children have done on the day that uses linking words and phrases. [5 marks max]
6. Accept any short paragraph about what the children plan to do the following week that uses linking words and phrases. [5 marks max]

Support, embed & challenge

Support

Use Grammar Unit 4 Resource 1: Finding connections to support children to identify and become more familiar with linking words and phrases that help readers see connections between sentences and clauses. Ask children to read the words and phrases in the grid, and colour the boxes that contain linking words and phrases. Afterwards, clarify which words are linking words. Cut these out and place them in a hat. Provide the children with a story opener, such as 'Seb was walking down the road when an alien spaceship landed in front of him.' Ask the children to take turns to take a word from the hat and use it to continue the story, with help from the rest of the group. Encourage them to use additional sentences before their linking word if necessary. (**Answers** Linking words and phrases: in the beginning, because, after that, because of this, now, so, next, but, as a result, finally)

Embed

Use Grammar Unit 4 Resource 2: Making it flow to enable the children to practice using linking words and phrases to connect the ideas within a pre-written paragraph about a theatre trip. Ask the children to read the sentences and add their own connecting adverbials or conjunctions into the gaps. (**Possible answers** 1. To begin with; 2. Then; 3. So; 4. Finally; 5. because; 6. quickly; 7. Next; 8. and; 9. After that; 10. Lastly)

Challenge

Challenge to children to imagine they are writing a longer report about something that interests them – it could be a book or television programme they enjoy or something they have learned at school. Tell them to write the first paragraph of their report, using linking words and phrases to show how their ideas are connected.

Homework / Additional activities

Ask children to select a few pages from a book they are currently reading. Ask them to find and note examples of linking words and phrases.

Collins Connect: Grammar Unit 4

Ask the children to complete Grammar Unit 4 (see Teach → Year 5 → Vocabulary, Grammar and Punctuation → Grammar Unit 4).

Grammar Unit 5A: Adverbials of time

Overview

English curriculum objectives
- Linking ideas across paragraphs using adverbials of time (for example: 'later'), place (for example: 'nearby'), and number (for example: 'secondly') or tense choices (for example: 'he had seen her before')

Treasure House resources
- Vocabulary, Grammar and Punctuation Skills Pupil Book 5, Grammar Unit 5A, pages 27–28
- Collins Connect Treasure House Vocabulary, Grammar and Punctuation Year 5, Grammar Unit 5
- Photocopiable Grammar Unit 5A, Resource 1: Last month at the farm, page 85
- Photocopiable Grammar Unit 5A, Resource 2: When did that happen? page 86

Introduction

Teaching overview
The next four units build on the children's prior knowledge of adverbs and adverbials by introducing the concept of adverbials of time (Unit 5A), place (Unit 5B), manner (Unit 5C) and number (Unit 5D).

Introduce the concept
Ask the children: What is an adverb? Elicit ideas and establish that an adverb is a word that adds meaning to a verb. Adverbs can tell you how, when or where the verb was happening. Tell the children that in this lesson they will learn about adverbials of time. Adverbials of time can show when and for how long things happen. They can often be put in different positions in the sentence to give different emphasis.

They can be single words (adverbs) or adverbial phrases. Write the following examples on the board to demonstrate:
- <u>Every day</u>, Jill tidies her bedroom.
- I'll tidy my room <u>tomorrow</u>.

Challenge the children, in their groups, to draw up a list of adverbials of time – reminding them that they can be words or phrases. Afterwards, gather together all the children's ideas into a class list, for example: 'now', 'then', 'after', 'soon', 'secondly', 'on Friday', 'as soon as possible', 'this afternoon', 'now and then', 'a few days later', 'once upon a time', 'in the beginning', 'one morning in June' and 'a week last Thursday'.

Pupil practice

Pupil Book pages 27–28

Get started
Ask the children to copy out the sentences and underline the adverbials of time. Afterwards, ask them to work with a partner to replace verbally the adverbial of time with a new one.

Answers
1. <u>Last month</u>, Katka's family moved house. [example]
2. <u>After the move</u>, they discovered some problems with the plumbing. [1 mark]
3. <u>For three days</u>, the family had no hot water. [1 mark]
4. Dad said the plumber was coming to fix the leak <u>on Saturday</u>. [1 mark]
5. But then he postponed <u>until a few days later</u>. [1 mark]
6. <u>Every day</u>, the family had to heat water on the stove. [1 mark]
7. The plumber <u>eventually</u> arrived and managed to solve the problem. [1 mark]
8. <u>By the following week</u>, Katka's family was relieved to have hot water again! [1 mark]

Try these
Ask the children to copy and complete the sentences by adding suitable adverbials of time from the box. The first answer has been completed as an example. Some of the answers have more than one possibility.

Answers
1. *I am going to stay with my grandparents for a week.* [example]
2. Yesterday [1 mark]
3. Last year [1 mark]
4. now [1 mark]
5. since Monday [1 mark]
6. finally [1 mark]

43

Grammar Unit 5A: Adverbials of time

Now try these
Ask the children to copy and expand the sentences by adding an adverbial of time. You may wish to support children by discussing their sentences before setting them to work independently.

Answers
Open-ended questions: Accept any adverbial phrases appropriate for the given sentences.

[1 mark per question]

Support, embed & challenge

Support
Cut out the sentences from Grammar Unit 5A Resource 2: When did that happen? and put them in a hat. Work with these children in a group and ask the children to take turns to take out a sentence and read it to the group. Ask them: 'When did that happen?' Take their answer and use it to model a sentence with an adverbial phrase. If using a fronted adverbial, remember out loud to place a comma after the adverbial. Once all the sentences have been written, ask these children to complete Grammar Unit 5A Resource 1: Last month at the farm to help them to recognise and identify adverbials of time. (**Answers** 1. time; 2. time; 3. place; 4. time; 5. place; 6. time; 7. place; 8. place; 9. time; 10. time) Ask them to add the adverbials on the sheet to the displayed class list.

Embed
Leaving the class list of adverbials displayed, ask the children to complete Grammar Unit 5A Resource 2: When did that happen? to provide practice in using adverbials of time to show when and for how long things happen. Afterwards, ask the children to search for as many examples of adverbials of time in their reading book as they can, adding the phrases to the class list. Now that the children are beginning to see the infinite possibilities of the adverbial of time, challenge them to create five more adverbial phrases that are not on the list already.

Challenge
Challenge these children to write really dramatic or poetic adverbial phrases, such as 'before the axe fell' or 'as the moon rose above the Jolly Roger'. Encourage them to experiment with combining adverbial phrases, such as 'On Saturday night, as the sun began to set' and so on.

Homework / Additional activities

Ask the children to write a paragraph about a family that moves away from a busy city to live on a remote farm, using adverbials of time to provide flow.

Collins Connect: Grammar Unit 5
Ask the children to complete Grammar Unit 5 (see Teach → Year 5 → Vocabulary, Grammar and Punctuation → Grammar Unit 5).

You might choose to use this unit to introduce adverbials or to use it as a recap after Unit 5D below.

Grammar Unit 5B: Adverbials of place

Overview

English curriculum objectives
- Linking ideas across paragraphs using adverbials of time (for example: 'later'), 'place' (for example: 'nearby'), and number (for example: 'secondly') or tense choices (for example: 'he had seen her before')

Treasure House resources
- Vocabulary, Grammar and Punctuation Skills Pupil Book 5, Grammar Unit 5B, pages 29–30
- Collins Connect Treasure House Vocabulary, Grammar and Punctuation Year 5, Grammar Unit 5
- Photocopiable Grammar Unit 5B, Resource 1: Over the hill and far away, page 87
- Photocopiable Grammar Unit 5B, Resource 2: Where did he go? page 88

Introduction

Teaching overview
This unit builds on the previous unit (Unit 5A) on adverbials of time to introduce adverbials of place. Adverbial phrases act like an adverb, providing more information about a verb or a clause. Adverbial phrases can be used at any point in a sentence, but a fronted adverbial (at the front of a sentence) can be very effective.

Introduce the concept
Briefly recap children's knowledge of adverbial phrases and clauses. Remind children that these can act as an adverb to give you more information about how, when or where something was happening. Explain that in this lesson they will learn about adverbials of place. Adverbials of place can show where things happen. They can sometimes be put in different positions in the sentence to give different emphasis but they often come after the main verb. They can be single words (adverbs) or adverbial phrases. Write the following examples on the board to demonstrate:
- Jack and Jill walked up the hill.
- Under a tree, they stopped and looked around.
- Using the same format as last unit, ask the children in their groups to write a list of adverbials of place. Encourage them to think widely and creatively. Use the ideas to create a class list for the children to use in their activities.

Pupil practice

Pupil Book pages 29–30

Get started
Ask the children to copy out the sentences and underline the adverbials of place. Afterwards, ask them to work with a partner to think of an alternative adverbial of place for each sentence.

Answers
1. *Katka's family moved to a large stone farmhouse in the countryside.* [example]
2. Katka really loves living at the farm. [1 mark]
3. Nearby, there is a village shop. [1 mark]
4. At the end of the lane, there is a sparkling stream full of little fish. [1 mark]
5. Katka looked around but she couldn't find the cycle path. [1 mark]
6. She searched everywhere she could think of. [1 mark]
7. It was a blustery day and the wind was blowing her sideways. [1 mark]
8. She decided she would travel westwards another day. [1 mark]

Try these
Ask the children to copy and complete each sentence by adding adverbials of place from the box. The first answer has been completed as an example.

Answers
1. *The children can run wild outside.* [example]
2. John looked everywhere but he couldn't see his friends. [1 mark]
3. "Look for the ball over there," shouted Deanna. [1 mark]
4. The rabbits are happy hopping around. [1 mark]
5. Nearby, the birds are splashing in the birdbath. [1 mark]
6. "Come back!" called Mum to the wild children. [1 mark]

Grammar Unit 5B: Adverbials of place

Now try these
Ask the children to copy and expand the sentences by adding adverbials of place. You may wish to support children by discussing their sentences before setting them to work independently.

Answers
Open-ended questions: Accept any adverbial phrases appropriate for the given sentences.

[1 mark per question]

Support, embed & challenge

Support
Work as a group to cut out and sort the words and phrases on Grammar Unit 5B Resource 1: Over the hill and far away. Afterwards, place the adverbials of place in the centre of the group and take turns to choose a phrase and use it in a sentence. Demonstrate how some of the phrases could go together and challenge the children to use two in the same sentence.

Make some simple sentences such as 'he sat' or 'she walked'. As a group take turns to add more and more exciting adverbials to each, for example: 'he sat under a tree', 'he sat on the rollercoaster' and 'he sat on the back of a flying elephant'. (**Answers** Adverbials of place: up the hill, back, under a tree, around, eastwards, at the farm, in the city, everywhere, nearby, at the end of the road, over there; Adverbials of manner: patiently, beautifully, quickly, anxiously, carefully, clumsily, bravely, sideways, greedily)

Embed
Ask the children to carry out the 'Support' activity above in pairs. Ask them to write a list of sentences starting 'he sat' or 'she walked', making the adverbial phrases more and more alarming from 'She walked to school' to 'she walked along the edge of the spitting volcano'.

Ask the children to complete Grammar Unit 5B Resource 2: Where did he go? to provide practice in using adverbials of place to show where things happen. Ask children to read the sentences then rewrite them, expanding them with an adverbial of place. Encourage them to make each one a small work of literature.

Challenge
Challenge these children to write a simple story in the style of *Bears in the Night* by Stan and Jan Berenstain (HarperCollins) or the traditional story 'In a dark, dark wood' in which a story is based around a build-up of adverbial phrases.

Homework / Additional activities
Ask children to write three sentences about a storm using adverbials of place.

Collins Connect: Grammar Unit 5
Ask the children to complete Grammar Unit 5 (see Teach → Year 5 → Vocabulary, Grammar and Punctuation → Grammar Unit 5).

You might choose to use this unit to introduce adverbials or to use it as a recap after Unit 5D below.

Grammar Unit 5C: Adverbials of manner

Overview

English curriculum objectives
- Linking ideas across paragraphs using adverbials of time (for example: 'later'), place (for example: 'nearby'), and number (for example: 'secondly') or tense choices (for example: 'he had seen her before')

Treasure House resources
- Vocabulary, Grammar and Punctuation Skills Pupil Book 5, Grammar Unit 5C, pages 31–32
- Collins Connect Treasure House Vocabulary, Grammar and Punctuation Year 5, Grammar Unit 5
- Photocopiable Grammar Unit 5C, Resource 1: Sentences with style, page 89
- Photocopiable Grammar Unit 5C, Resource 2: How did she do that? page 90

Introduction

Teaching overview
This unit builds on the previous units on adverbials of time (Unit 5A) and adverbials of place (Unit 5B) to introduce adverbials of manner. Adverbial phrases act like an adverb, providing more information about a verb or a clause. Adverbial phrases can be used at any point in a sentence, but a fronted adverbial (at the front of a sentence) can be particularly effective.

Introduce the concept
Explain to the children that adverbials of manner can show how things happen. They can sometimes be put in different positions in the sentence to give different emphasis, but they often come after the main verb. They can be single words (adverbs) or adverbial phrases. Write the following examples on the board to demonstrate:

- Jack and Jill walked <u>quickly</u>.
- David <u>carefully</u> unwrapped his present.

Provide the children working in their groups with the following adverbial phrases: 'with enthusiasm', 'like a whirlwind', 'as carefully as possible' and 'kindly', and ask them to write a sentence for each on mini whiteboards and hold them up. Share the examples and model changing the place of the adverbial to create different effects.

Pupil practice

Pupil Book pages 31–32

Get started
Ask the children to copy the sentences and underline the adverbials of manner. Afterwards, as a class, discuss different adverbs or adverbials that could replace the underlined words.

Answers
1. The children played the instruments <u>with gusto</u>. [example]
2. The teacher <u>patiently</u> smiled at them. [1 mark]
3. Sara blew the trumpet <u>as if her life depended on it</u>. [1 mark]
4. Heather tried her best to sing <u>beautifully</u>. [1 mark]
5. The parents watched the concert <u>anxiously</u>. [1 mark]
6. Karl banged the drums <u>hard and fast</u>. [1 mark]
7. The teacher <u>bravely</u> soldiered on. [1 mark]
8. At the end of the concert the head teacher approached the stage <u>nervously</u>. [1 mark]

Try these
Ask the children to copy and complete each sentence by adding the most suitable adverbial of manner from the box. The first answer has been completed as an example.

Answers
1. Anna ate her lunch <u>in silence</u>. [example]
2. Liam shoved his things in his bag <u>roughly</u>. [1 mark]
3. Jamila <u>angrily</u> stomped down the path. [1 mark]
4. Frances crept up on her sister <u>slowly</u>. [1 mark]
5. The teacher <u>happily</u> announced home time. [1 mark]
6. Fabian stroked the guinea pig <u>very gently</u>. [1 mark]

Grammar Unit 5C: Adverbials of manner

Now try these
Ask the children to copy and expand the sentences by adding an adverbial of manner. You may wish to support children by reading the sentences together before setting them to work independently.

Answers
Open-ended questions: Accept any adverbial phrases appropriate for the given sentences. [1 mark per question]

Support, embed & challenge

Support
Recap on the use of adverbs using simple sentences such as 'she walked'. Challenge the children working around the group to add an adverb to the sentence, asking them to act out the sentence they created. Play the game on Grammar Unit 5C Resource 1: Sentences with style as a group to support the children in becoming more familiar and more confident with adverbials of manner that show how things can happen. As the children develop their confidence, encourage two or three children to each create a different sentence for the word or phrase indicated by the dice.

Embed
Ask these children to work in pairs to create a list of 10 different adverbs or adverbial phrases of manner. Ask them to join with another pair and copy down any new words and phrases.

Ask the children to complete Grammar Unit 5C Resource 2: How did she do that? to enable children to practice using adverbials of manner within sentences, then moving on to combine adverbials of time and manner. Encourage the children to use a correctly punctuated fronted adverbial in some of their sentences.

Challenge
Challenge the children to add an adverbial of time, an adverbial of place and an adverbial of manner to each of the sentence on Grammar Unit 5C Resource 2: How did she do that?

Homework / Additional activities

Ask the children to write a paragraph about a family that visits a mountain climbing holiday resort. Tell children to use examples of adverbials of manner in their writing.

Collins Connect: Grammar Unit 5
Ask the children to complete Grammar Unit 5 (see Teach → Year 5 → Vocabulary, Grammar and Punctuation → Grammar Unit 5).

You might choose to use this unit to introduce adverbials or to use it as a recap after Unit 5D below.

Grammar Unit 5D: Adverbials of number

Overview

English curriculum objectives
- Linking ideas across paragraphs using adverbials of time (for example: 'later'), place (for example: 'nearby'), and number (for example: 'secondly' or tense choices (for example: 'he *had* seen her before')

Treasure House resources
- Vocabulary, Grammar and Punctuation Skills Pupil Book 5, Grammar Unit 5D, pages 33–34
- Collins Connect Treasure House Vocabulary, Grammar and Punctuation Year 5, Grammar Unit 5
- Photocopiable Grammar Unit 5D, Resource 1: Adverbials of number game, page 91
- Photocopiable Grammar Unit 5D, Resource 2: How often? page 92

Additional resources
- The following phrases on separate cards: up the hill, down the lane, in the woods, on the way to school, far away, around the corner, nearby, anxiously, genuinely, in a flash, with a heavy heart, like thunder, with panache, as fast as she could, spectacularly badly, always, four times a week, seldom, twice a day, once a year, first, on Monday, for three days, after

Introduction

Teaching overview
This unit builds on the previous units on adverbials of time (Unit 5A), adverbials of place (Unit 5B) and adverbials of manner (Unit 5C) to introduce adverbials of number. Adverbial phrases act like an adverb, providing more information about a verb or a clause. Adverbial phrases can be used at any point in a sentence, but a fronted adverbial (at the front of a sentence) can be particularly effective.

Introduce the concept
Recap on adverbials of time, place and manner, challenging the children to give you an example of each.

Explain that adverbials of number can show how many times and in which order things happen.

These are very similar to adverbials of time, but all these adverbials have a direct link to a number. Remind children that adverbs and adverbials can be used in different places in a sentence and if they are at the beginning of a sentence, they need a comma:

- <u>First</u>, Tina phoned her friend.
- I walk the dog <u>twice a day</u>.

Place four poster-sized pieces of paper on four different tables. Label them: 'Time', 'Place', 'Manner' and 'Number'. Organise the children into pairs and challenge them to write an adverbial phrase or an adverb on each sheet of paper, trying not to repeat any words or phrases already there. Pin up the sheets at the front of the room and read the posters together. Highlight any particularly fine phrases.

Pupil practice

Pupil Book pages 33–34

Get started
Ask the children to copy the sentences and underline the adverbials of number. Together, suggest alternative adverbials of number that could be used in the sentence instead.

Answers

1. The postman brings the post <u>once a day</u>. [example]
2. <u>Four times a week</u>, I train for the swimming competition. [1 mark]
3. <u>Secondly</u>, I can't meet you at that time. [1 mark]
4. I have only met my great uncle <u>once</u>. [1 mark]
5. Mary went to the library <u>three times this month</u>. [1 mark]
6. Ursula <u>always</u> plans ahead. [1 mark]
7. I <u>seldom</u> go to that part of town. [1 mark]
8. <u>Lastly</u>, I'd like to visit the aquarium. [1 mark]

Try these
Ask the children to copy and complete each sentence by adding the most suitable adverbial of number from the box. The first answer has been completed as an example. Some of the answers have more than one possibility.

Answers

1. I brush my teeth <u>twice</u> a day. [example]
2. We went to the cinema <u>first</u>. [1 mark]

Grammar Unit 5D: Adverbials of number

3. <u>Once</u> I saw a heron at the side of the canal. [1 mark]
4. I watched my favourite film <u>three times</u> in a row! [1 mark]
5. <u>Secondly</u>, I would like to talk about the rules. [1 mark]
6. <u>Lastly</u>, let me tell you about the end of the show. [1 mark]

Now try these
Ask the children to copy and expand the sentences by adding an adverbial of number. You may wish to support children by reading the sentences together before setting them to work independently.

Answers
Open-ended questions: Accept any adverbial phrases appropriate for the given sentences.

[1 mark per question]

Support, embed & challenge

Support
Support the children as they play the game on Grammar Unit 5D Resource 1: Adverbials of number game, in pairs or individually, to become more familiar with adverbials of number.

Put all the phrase cards (see Additional resources) in a hat and ask the children to take turns to pull a card from the hat and read it. As a group, they decide what sort of adverbial it is. Then they should work together on a piece of shared writing, to write a sentence for the word, trying out different positions for the adverbials.

Embed
Ask the children to complete Grammar Unit 5D Resource 2: How often? to practice expanding sentences using more than one adverbial phrase

Give the children, working in threes, a set of the phrases (see Additional resources) and a hat to put them in. Ask the children to take turns to pull out a phrase and read it aloud. The other two children in the group must race each other to say a sentence that uses the phrase.

Challenge
Challenge the children to create posters that demonstrate how adverbials of number can add additional information to a sentence.

Challenge these children to add three adverbial phrases to each of the sentences on Grammar Unit 5D Resource 2: How often?

Homework / Additional activities
Ask children to write a paragraph about themselves detailing the things that they do and how often.

Collins Connect: Grammar Unit 5
Ask the children to complete Grammar Unit 5 (see Teach → Year 5 → Vocabulary, Grammar and Punctuation → Grammar Unit 5).

Review unit 2: Grammar

Pupil Book pages 35–36

A. Ask children to rewrite each sentence in more formal language. Accept any suitable answer.

Example answers

1. I am so pleased that we are visiting Devon on Saturday. [1 mark]
2. Could you tell me if you are going to the football match on Friday? [1 mark]
3. Please can you contact me to let me know where we will be meeting. [1 mark]
4. Would you like to visit me tomorrow. I will be at home all day. [1 mark]
5. What will you be doing on Tuesday afternoon? [1 mark]

B. Ask the children to answer the questions with two sentences, one using a modal verb and one using an adverb, to show how likely the actions of the verbs are. Accept any suitable answer.

Example answers

1. Yes, I might go tomorrow. [1 mark]
   Yes, I'll probably go tomorrow. [1 mark]
2. I will be going to Tilly's party. [1 mark]
   I am definitely going to Tilly's party. [1 mark]
3. No, I should do something but I'm not. [1 mark]
   I don't want to, but my mum will probably make me do something. [1 mark]
4. I would love to climb Mount Everest. [1 mark]
   Perhaps I will climb Mount Everest when I'm older. [1 mark]
5. We shall go camping in Wales. [1 mark]
   We are possibly going camping in Wales. [1 mark]

C. Ask children to copy out the sentences, underlining the relative clause in each.

Answers

1. Nottingham is a famous city <u>where tourists often visit.</u> [1 mark]
2. This is the jacket <u>that I bought</u>. [1 mark]
3. Denise handed her earrings, <u>which were gold hoops</u>, to her swimming teacher. [1 mark]
4. Sonja, <u>who lives with her aunt</u>, is coming to tea. [1 mark]
5. It was almost 9:10 p.m. <u>when the show started</u>. [1 mark]

D. Ask children to copy and complete the sentences by adding connecting adverbials or conjunctions to create a paragraph about a fishing trip. Accept any suitable answers.

Example answers

1. Early on Monday morning, we got all our kit ready to go then we loaded up the van. [1 mark]
2. We stopped on the way because I wanted a drink. [1 mark]
3. We ate our picnic by the river. [1 mark]
4. First, we tried our luck fishing in the big lake. [1 mark]
5. After a wonderful day, we went home jubilant because we caught the prize! [1 mark]

E. Ask children to copy and expand these sentences, putting one adverbial of time and one adverbial of place in each. Accept any suitable answers.

Example answers

1. On the first day of June, Debbie spring-cleaned her cottage in the country. [1 mark]
2. There was always a lot of dust and dirt everywhere. [1 mark]
3. She worked hard all day cleaning and tidying from top to bottom. [1 mark]
4. At the end of the day, Debbie was pleased with her efforts throughout the cottage. [1 mark]
5. In the evening light, she sat down to eat a piece of cake and drink a cup of tea in the garden. [1 mark]

Punctuation Unit 1: Using commas for clearer meaning

Overview

English curriculum objectives
- Use of commas to clarify meaning or avoid ambiguity in writing

Treasure House resources
- Vocabulary, Grammar and Punctuation Skills Pupil Book 5, Punctuation Unit 1, pages 37–38
- Collins Connect Treasure House Vocabulary, Grammar and Punctuation Year 5, Punctuation Unit 1
- Photocopiable Punctuation Unit 1, Resource 1: Comma quiz page 93
- Photocopiable Punctuation Unit 1, Resource 2: Commas galore, page 94

Introduction

Teaching overview
This unit focuses on using commas to make sentences clearer or less ambiguous. The use of many or very few commas will become a personal preference as the children develop their own writing style, but they should be encouraged to use commas to ensure that the words they write reflect what they want to say. Commas can be very useful in clarifying meaning as well as helping the reader to easily read the text.

Introduce the concept
Explain to the children that commas can be useful to make the meaning of sentences clearer. They show small breaks between words, phrases or clauses.

We also use them to separate items in lists. Write the following examples on the board:
- Can we eat Granny?
- We need chocolate biscuits and an apple.
- Please go and help John.

Ask the children to tell you what the sentences mean. Now write on the board:
- Can we eat, Granny?
- We need chocolate, biscuits and an apple.
- Please go and help, John.

Ask the children to turn to a partner and discuss how the comma changes the meaning of each sentence.

Pupil practice

Pupil Book pages 37–38

Get started
Ask the children to copy and complete the sentences by adding commas. You may wish to support the children by reading each sentence aloud and then pausing while they find and point to the places that need commas, before asking them to copy the sentences.

Answers
1. *I would like to visit Norway, Poland and Latvia.* [example]
2. To bake a cake you need eggs, flour and sugar. [1 mark]
3. To be safe on a climbing trip you should take a friend, ropes and water. [1 mark]
4. Some of the chores you could do include tidying, vacuuming and polishing. [1 mark]
5. An ancient pirate treasure chest could contain gold, silver and emeralds. [1 mark]
6. At school today, we learned lots of new skills in Maths, English and Science. [1 mark]
7. My favourite sports clubs to attend after school are tennis, zumba and athletics. [1 mark]
8. Before I can go to bed, I have to practice my drumming, spelling and times tables. [1 mark]

Try these
Ask the children to copy and complete each sentence by adding a comma after the adverbial. The first answer has been completed as an example.

Answers
1. *When I am older, I would like to travel all around the world.* [example]
2. Every Thursday, I bake a cake to take to my book club. [1 mark]
3. If the weather gets better, I might go climbing this weekend. [1 mark]
4. When I need some extra money, I do more chores around the house. [1 mark]
5. Even though I've spent a long time looking, I've never found any of the treasure. [1 mark]
6. With a sudden rush, my cousin bolted into the room. [1 mark]
7. Under the sofa, we found the model car I had lost last year. [1 mark]
8. Twice a day, I make sure I brush my teeth. [1 mark]

Punctuation Unit 1: Using commas for clearer meaning

Now try these

Remind the children of their previous work on relative clauses, then ask them to copy and complete the sentences by adding commas around the relative clauses. You may wish to support children by discussing their sentences before setting them to work independently.

Answers

1. *The pirate, whose loot we were hunting, was catching up with us.* [example]
2. It all started when some diamonds, which were incredibly valuable, had gone missing. [1 mark]
3. In a moment, when I hadn't even been concentrating, I'd worked out where they must be. [1 mark]
4. My quest, which was very risky, was to track them. [1 mark]
5. The sea captain with me, who was new to the job, was nervous. [1 mark]
6. Lost Island, where the jewels were buried, seemed deserted. [1 mark]

Support, embed & challenge

Support

Use Punctuation Unit 1 Resource 1: Comma quiz to enable children to revise and consolidate the content from the unit.

Write the following sentences on slips of paper and read them with the children:

- Make sure you're watching Billy.
- Don't forget to say thank you Lisa.
- Ravi says Tina hit him.
- Make sure you're watching, Billy.
- Don't forget to say thank you, Lisa.
- Ravi, says Tina, hit him.

Pair up the matching sentences and compare the meaning of each. Clarify that neither is wrong, as long as that is what the writing means (though we might want to put some inverted commas around 'thank you Lisa'). (**Answers** 1. true; 2. true; 3. false; 4. true; 5. false; 6. false)

Embed

Ask the children to carry out the activity Punctuation Unit 1 Resource 2: Commas galore. This will enable children to gain confidence in using commas in lists, for fronted adverbials and around relative clauses. (**Answers** 1. Mum says I must put my laundry away, tidy my desk and take my empty cups to the kitchen.; 2. Today, we baked gingerbread biscuits, chocolate chip cookies, shortbread and a Victoria sponge.; 3. At the car show I saw a funny red sports car, a huge green tractor, a flashy blue motorbike and a silver Rolls Royce.; 4. Next Thursday, we are moving house.; 5. After a very long time away, the giant finally returned home.; 6. With a sudden flash, the skies turned black and rain lashed down.; 7. My friend, who is an excellent writer, has nearly finished writing a whole book.; 8. It all started when a strange parcel, that was small and rectangular, arrived in the post.; 9. My job, which was terribly important, was to protect the treasure map at all costs.; 10. I am going to make us a snack of ice-cream, soda and crisps.)

Write the following on the board and ask the children, in pairs, to write out the sentences and add commas to match the meaning.

- My favourite things are cooking rabbits and princess. (Meaning: my favourite things are cooking and rabbits and princesses.)
- Ask your cousin Jake if he wants a baked potato. (Meaning: Jake, can you ask your cousin if he wants a baked potato.)

Challenge

Challenge the children to write four silly sentences, modelled on the sentences in this unit, that are missing their commas. Share these sentences with the rest of the class and ask the children to punctuate them.

Homework / Additional activities

Ask the children to write a short story about some friends who go on an adventure to try to find a pirate's treasure chest. Tell them to use at least one example of commas in a list, at least one example of a comma after a fronted adverbial and at least one example of commas around a relative clause.

Collins Connect: Punctuation Unit 1

Ask the children to complete Punctuation Unit 1 (see Teach → Year 5 → Vocabulary, Grammar and Punctuation → Punctuation Unit 1).

Punctuation Unit 2: Hyphens

Overview

English curriculum objectives
- How hyphens can be used to avoid ambiguity [for example: 'man eating shark' versus 'man-eating shark', or 'recover' versus 're-cover']

Treasure House resources
- Vocabulary, Grammar and Punctuation Skills Pupil Book 5, Punctuation Unit 2, pages 39–40
- Collins Connect Treasure House Vocabulary, Grammar and Punctuation Year 5, Punctuation Unit 2

- Photocopiable Punctuation Unit 2, Resource 1: Compound adjective generator, page 95
- Photocopiable Punctuation Unit 2, Resource 2: The super-useful hyphen, page 96

Additional resources
- The following words on cards: playtime, playground, goalkeeper, outdoors, newspaper, prizewinner, classroom, sunset, hairbrush, English-speaking, well-known, mouth-watering, full-length, twenty-paged, blue-green, seldom-seen

Introduction

Teaching overview
This unit looks at the use of hyphens to avoid ambiguity in writing. The children will have already covered using hyphens to avoid ambiguity when writing some words with prefixes in their Spelling programme. This unit covers using hyphens for compound adjectives. In this unit, the children will first spend time clarifying the difference between compound nouns that do not need a hyphen, and compound adjectives that do.

Introduce the concept
Tell the children that compound words are words made from two or more shorter words. They have one unit of meaning. Compound nouns do not usually have a hyphen (-), for example: 'A <u>football</u> is a ball you kick with your foot.'

We do, however, use hyphens to join words that make compound adjectives, for example: 'The <u>man-eating</u> crocodile lurked on the bank of the deep river.' 'The <u>rosy-cheeked</u> children sang and danced in the park.'

Provide each group of children with a set of the word cards (see Additional resources) and ask them to sort them into nouns and adjectives. Together, draw up a list of all the words on the board in two columns and locate the hyphens used in the compound adjectives. Challenge each table to write a sentence for one of the compound adjectives. Ask volunteers to come and write these on the board.

Look again at the two lists. Help the children to see that the compound nouns are objects, or ideas, that tend to be well-known or established. Some of the compound adjectives are well-established words but many will be unique to the sentence. Encourage the children to be creative – but accurate – in using these words.

Pupil practice

Pupil Book pages 39–40

Get started
Ask the children to copy the sentences and underline the compound word in each one. You may wish to support the children by reading each sentence aloud, then pausing while they find and point to the compound word, before asking them to copy the sentences.

Answers
1. At <u>playtime</u>, this morning, our teacher said he had an exciting new scheme to challenge us. [example]
2. He said the school had won some money and asked us to design a new school <u>playground</u>. [1 mark]
3. For the last two years, I have been the <u>goalkeeper</u> in our school team. [1 mark]
4. Therefore, of course, I designed a large grassy area to act as a huge <u>football</u> pitch. [1 mark]
5. The day they revealed the winner, we had a great party <u>outdoors</u> with music and cakes. [1 mark]
6. A <u>newspaper</u> reporter came to report on the event. [1 mark]
7. She wanted to conduct an interview with the <u>prizewinner</u>. [1 mark]
8. The winning design, which was not mine, included a big <u>classroom</u> space in the fresh air. [1 mark]

Punctuation Unit 2: Hyphens

Try these
Ask the children to look at each pair of phrases and copy out the phrases that use hyphens correctly. The first answer has been completed as an example.

Answers

1. *the short-sighted man*	[example]
2. our city-centre school	[1 mark]
3. pretty gold hair	[1 mark]
4. the kind-hearted girl	[1 mark]
5. the kind old man	[1 mark]
6. one two-year-old child	[1 mark]
7. the dish-washing sponge	[1 mark]
8. a happy-go-lucky smile	[1 mark]

Now try these
Ask the children to change each phrase into a description that uses a hyphenated compound adjective. Then they use it in a sentence.

Answers

1. quick-drying paint	[1 mark]
2. a brown-spotted cow	[1 mark]
3. a three-legged mouse	[1 mark]
4. a fire-eating man	[1 mark]
5. a yellow-feathered bird	[1 mark]
6. a long-necked lizard	[1 mark]

Support, embed & challenge

Support
Return to the words in the Get started activity. Re-sort a set of the words and again establish the difference between the words. Challenge the children to think of some more compound words: 'snowman', 'doorstep', 'goalkeeper', 'chairlift', 'fireman' and so on. Write these on a whiteboard. Now share the words in Punctuation Unit 2, Resource 1: Compound adjective generator. Cut out the words and place them face up. Ask the children to take turns to find two words that can be combined to form a compound adjective. Start pairing up the words and encouraging the children to make up sentences for the words they have created, attempting to write these on mini whiteboards.

Embed
Ask these children to use Punctuation Unit 2 Resource 2: The super-useful hyphen to practice locating words that need hyphenating. (**Answers** 1. Sir George ran away from the fire-breathing dragon as fast as he could.; 2. Corry jumped into the ice-cold water.; 3. I have got to babysit my irritating four-year-old cousin this afternoon.; 4. The garden had become overgrown in the warm, wet mid-June weather.; 5. My great-grandfather is ninety-six years old.; 6. The sea was a stormy grey-green and the wind whipped around the already-cold tourists.; 7. Mina ate the day-old sandwiches and drank the funny-tasting milk.; 8. Nile felt silly in his too-small jumper and too-short trousers.; 9. There are many strange-looking creatures at the bottom of the deepest part of the ocean.; 10. We ate ice-creams at the beach and put T-shirts on our already-burned arms.)

Ask the children to write their own sentences using compound adjectives: ask them to use the sentences on the resource sheet as a starting point (writing their own versions) or provide them with Punctuation Unit 2 Resource 1: Compound adjective generator and ask them to find words to use there.

Challenge
Challenge the children to rewrite a section from a book they are reading, changing descriptions such as 'the man with the fair hair' into phrases with hyphenated compound adjectives ('the fair-haired man'). They should think about the effect they are creating when they write using lots of hyphenated words.

Homework / Additional activities

Ask the children to write a short paragraph that describes either a bright colourful house – where each of the rooms is a different colour – or someone wearing an outfit of many colours. Encourage them to focus on creating some interesting colours: blue-green, fiery-orange and so on.

Collins Connect: Punctuation Unit 2
Ask the children to complete Punctuation Unit 2 (see Teach → Year 5 → Vocabulary, Grammar and Punctuation → Punctuation Unit 2).

Punctuation Unit 3: Brackets, dashes and commas

Overview

English curriculum objectives
- Using brackets, dashes or commas to indicate parenthesis

Treasure House resources
- Vocabulary, Grammar and Punctuation Skills Pupil Book 5, Punctuation Unit 3, pages 41–42
- Collins Connect Treasure House Vocabulary, Grammar and Punctuation Year 5, Punctuation Unit 3
- Photocopiable Punctuation Unit 3, Resource 1: Parenthesis practice, page 97
- Photocopiable Punctuation Unit 3, Resource 2: Commas, brackets and dashes, page 98

Introduction

Teaching overview

This unit introduces children to the concept of using brackets, dashes and commas to separate extra detail in sentences, otherwise known as parenthesis. The children will have spent time this year using and punctuating embedded relative clauses in parenthesis and can now move on to putting relative clauses and then other clauses in brackets or – for a more modern look – dashes. In many cases the use of commas, brackets or dashes will be personal preference, but in some situations, for example with multiple asides, the use of brackets might be clearer.

Introduce the concept

Write the following examples on the board. Ask the children to locate the embedded relative clause and tell you how each one is different.

- The party (held in a posh hotel) was great.
- The party – held in a posh hotel – was great.
- The party, held in a posh hotel, was great.

Elicit ideas and establish that the words in the sentences are the same but that the punctuation used varies. Explain to the children that brackets, dashes and commas can all be used in a sentence to separate a word, phrase or clause that gives extra detail. This is called parenthesis. Ask the children which they prefer and whether they feel that the different punctuation gives a different feel. Perhaps the brackets give a stronger sense of an aside.

Write the following sentence on the board and ask partners to write it on their mini whiteboard, punctuate it according to their preference and hold it up.

Jacob who had not practiced played the keyboard badly in his lesson.

Discuss the punctuation the children have chosen.

Pupil practice

Pupil Book pages 41–42

Get started

Ask the children to copy out the sentences, underlining the parenthesis. You may wish to support the children by reading each list aloud, then pausing while they discuss and decide which part of the sentence is the parenthesis, before asking them to copy the sentences.

Answers

1. A photograph <u>(which showed the position of hidden treasure)</u> was discovered under the floorboards. [example]
2. The boy <u>– Dominic –</u> made a clever and daring plan. [1 mark]
3. He stowed away, <u>before anyone could see him</u>, on a ship. [1 mark]
4. The captain <u>(who was very clever, too)</u> discovered him. [1 mark]
5. Dominic told the captain <u>– who was utterly fascinated –</u> about the photograph. [1 mark]
6. Together, <u>and with the rest of the ship's crew</u>, they decided to set out in search of the treasure. [1 mark]
7. They had a long, hard journey <u>(which was to be expected)</u>, but they bore up well. [1 mark]
8. Finally <u>– just when they were giving up hope –</u> they saw land. [1 mark]

Try these

Ask the children to copy out the sentences, adding punctuation around the underlined examples of parenthesis. The first answer has been completed as an example. The punctuation marks used will vary.

Punctuation Unit 3: Brackets, dashes and commas

Answers
1. *The sea, with its cruel nature, had been unforgiving.* [example]
2. The island (which they had been seeking) was in the distance. [1 mark]
3. The ship disappeared – all of a sudden – into some thick fog. [1 mark]
4. The captain, who was looking around in confusion, was worried. [1 mark]
5. His crew (who had been right next to him) were now nowhere to be seen. [1 mark]
6. Then – with a great start – he heard his first mate's voice. [1 mark]
7. The first mate, a tall, strong man, was still close by. [1 mark]
8. When the fog cleared (finally blown away to sea) everyone could see what had happened. [1 mark]

Now try these
Ask the children to copy out the sentences, adding some extra information in parenthesis. The style of punctuation marks used and the content may vary.

Example answers
1. Our basketball game (last Tuesday) was ruined by a storm. [1 mark]
2. I am (with the help of my sister) planning a birthday party. [1 mark]
3. The new girl (who joined today) is sitting at my project table. [1 mark]
4. I was starving (and I mean starving) when I got home. [1 mark]
5. Maya would try to have (or definitely shall have) an early night. [1 mark]
6. The science exam (which I'm not looking forward to) will be held on Thursday morning. [1 mark]

Support, embed & challenge

Support
Use Punctuation Unit 3 Resource 1: Parenthesis practice with the children. Cut out the individual sentences and give a sentence to each pair of children. Ask them to find the part of the sentence they want to put into brackets. Ask them to underline and then cut out the clause they want to put in parenthesis and see if the rest of the sentence goes together. Share the sentences, writing them together on the whiteboard, asking the pair which punctuation they want to use. Provide the children with individual copies of the resource sheet and ask them to complete it. (**Answers** 1. A magazine article (written in 2013) revealed the secrets of the author's greatest book. 2. The girl (Sally Anne) decided she would try to be more helpful in future. 3. He ran and hid, before anyone had noticed he was gone, under the stairwell. 4. The teacher, who was very clever, tried the children's test and failed it. 5. Kieran told his aunt (who was shocked) about the discovery. 6. The children (with the help of Mr Edge the caretaker) set off towards the wooded area. 7. It had been a long day, which was normal for Wednesdays, but it was nearly home time. 8. Finally – at just after 5 p.m. – Heidi called. 9. The forest, with its collection of Nordic trees, was spookily inviting. 10. The cave (that they had been searching for all day) was finally visible in the distance.)

To emphasise the use of parenthesis further, ask the children to read out their punctuated sentences, putting up their hands to one side of their mouth and saying the phrase in parenthesis as if it were a secret.

Embed
Ask the children to complete Punctuation Unit 3 Resource 2: Commas, brackets and dashes to enable children to practice using parenthesis with more independence. Ask children to read the sentences then rewrite them, adding in their own parenthesis complete with punctuation marks.

Challenge
Challenge children to complete a parenthesis investigation: Tell children to use a selection of different books to look for examples of parenthesis. Discover whether authors show a preference for brackets, commas or dashes, or whether they use a mixture. Notice the effect of text that uses the different marks for parenthesis. Ask children to create a presentation of their findings to share with the class.

Homework / Additional activities
Challenge the children to try and find out if there is a rule for which parenthesis marks a writer should use.

Collins Connect: Punctuation Unit 3
Ask the children to complete Punctuation Unit 3 (see Teach → Year 5 → Vocabulary, Grammar and Punctuation → Punctuation Unit 3).

Punctuation Unit 4: Boundaries between clauses

Overview

English curriculum objectives
- Using the semicolon, colon and dash to mark the boundary between independent clauses (for example: 'It's raining; I'm fed up']

Treasure House resources
- Vocabulary, Grammar and Punctuation Skills Pupil Book 5, Punctuation Unit 4, pages 43–44
- Collins Connect Treasure House Vocabulary, Grammar and Punctuation Year 5, Punctuation Unit 4

- Photocopiable Punctuation Unit 4, Resource 1: Colon – semicolon – dash, page 99
- Photocopiable Punctuation Unit 4, Resource 2: After the dash, page 100

Additional resources
- The following phrases on cards: 'We couldn't play hockey because it was raining.' 'I read the latest book by Lauren Child and I really enjoyed it.' 'I am learning to play the guitar.' 'I'm going to be a pop star when I grow up.'

Introduction

Teaching overview
This unit explores how colons, semicolons and dashes are used to separate main clauses as alternatives to full stops or conjunctions.

Introduce the concept
Remind the children that you cannot separate two main clauses (a clause that can be as a sentence) with a comma, but sometimes we want to use something not as strong as a full stop. Explain to the children that we can use a colon, semicolon or dash to separate main clauses, instead of full stops or conjunctions. Semicolons show linked clauses that are equally important, for example (write on board to demonstrate):

- The school bus is usually late; it was late again today.

Colons introduce reasons or examples: we can use it instead of the word 'because'. For example (write on board to demonstrate):

- The school bus was late today: it had a flat tyre.

Dashes can be used instead, in informal writing. For example (write on board to demonstrate):

- The school bus was late – now we'll be late for school!

Provide the children with the sentences from Additional resources above. Ask them to punctuate them, using a colon, a semicolon or a dash, using a different one each time. Ask volunteers to write the newly punctuated sentences on the board.

Pupil practice

Pupil Book pages 43–44

Get started
Ask the children to copy out the example from each pair that is an independent clause. You may wish to support the children by reading each pair of examples aloud and then pausing while they discuss and decide upon which is the independent clause. The first answer has been completed as an example.

Answers

1. *There was a pram standing in the hall.* [example]
2. That is great! [1 mark]
3. My aunt and my little sister are finally back at home. [1 mark]
4. Sue-Ann was singing her song very loudly. [1 mark]
5. Louis arrived with his friend from the Scouts. [1 mark]
6. The desert island was beautiful. [1 mark]

Try these
Ask the children to copy and complete the sentences by adding a colon, semicolon or dash between the two independent clauses. Encourage them to read the sentence out loud so that they can hear the two clauses.

Example answers

1. *Mum had an idea: we could play a game.* [example]
2. Pavel grinned; he liked games. [1 mark]
3. He chose a red counter – I chose a green one. [1 mark]
4. Pavel was doing well; he kept rolling high numbers. [1 mark]
5. Then I caught up – I won! [1 mark]
6. We may play again; I'll be more confident next time. [1 mark]

Punctuation Unit 4: Boundaries between clauses

7. Perhaps Dad would like to play as well: he likes games too. [1 mark]

8. We should play outside now – though the weather has not cleared up. [1 mark]

Now try these

Ask the children to copy and complete the sentences by adding a suitable independent clause. Accept any appropriate independent clauses.

Example answers

1. They carried on: far into the distance. [1 mark]

2. The wind blew hard – we should've put our coats on. [1 mark]

3. The dog ran on ahead; I couldn't keep up with her. [1 mark]

4. A deer appeared beside them: it was a red deer. [1 mark]

5. They thought they would be OK – they got lost! [1 mark]

6. They finally got back to the town; they were back home at last. [1 mark]

Support, embed & challenge

Support

Look at the following sentences with these children.

> We walk to school. It's not far away.
>
> Josh plays hockey. He has a match on Thursday.
>
> The tomatoes grew well. The children watered them every day.
>
> We were late for school. Lars couldn't find his shoes.

As a group, discuss different ways of combining the sentences, for example: 'We walk to school – it's not far away.' 'Josh plays hockey: he has a match on Thursday.' 'The tomatoes grew well: the children watered them every day.'

When the children are ready, ask them to complete Punctuation Unit 4 Resource 1: Colon – semicolon – dash to clarify where, what and why they should use colons, semicolons or dashes between two independent clauses. Ask the children to answer the questions on the resource sheet. Then they read the sentences below and add the appropriate punctuation in the correct places. (**Answers** 1. to introduce reasons or examples; 2. to show linked clauses that are equally important; 3. in informal writing; 1. Kasey had a plan; she wanted to look in the loft.; 2. Mum frowned: the loft could be dangerous.; 3. Dad got the ladder out; Kasey got her torch.; 4. Kasey's torch wouldn't turn on: it had run out of battery.; 5. Dad fetched new batteries – Kasey was gone!; 6. The weather had turned sunny: Kasey wanted to make the most of it.)

Embed

Use Punctuation Unit 4 Resource 2: After the dash to enable children to become more confident in adding their own additional clauses after ones that are provided. Ask children to read the sentences and then complete them by adding their own independent clause after the punctuation.

Explain to the children that colons, semicolons and dashes can look very impressive in their writing. Ask the children to return to a complete piece of writing they have done recently and challenge them to find one place where they could use a semicolon, one place where they could use a colon and one place where they could use a dash.

Challenge

Challenge these children to search through a number of books and find examples of two main clauses being separated by a comma. Ask them to rewrite the clauses, connecting them with more appropriate punctuation.

Homework / Additional activities

Challenge the children to use books they are currently reading to find and copy six examples of sentences that use a colon, semicolon or dash to create a break between main clauses.

Collins Connect: Punctuation Unit 4

Ask the children to complete Punctuation Unit 4 (see Teach → Year 5 → Vocabulary, Grammar and Punctuation → Punctuation Unit 4).

Punctuation Unit 5: Colons to introduce lists

Overview

English curriculum objectives
- Use of the colon to introduce a list

Treasure House resources
- Vocabulary, Grammar and Punctuation Skills Pupil Book 5, Punctuation Unit 5, pages 45–46
- Collins Connect Treasure House Vocabulary, Grammar and Punctuation Year 5, Punctuation Unit 5
- Photocopiable Punctuation Unit 5, Resource 1: I love: cake, tea and more cake, page 101
- Photocopiable Punctuation Unit 5, Resource 2: Roll the dice, page 102

Introduction

Teaching overview
This unit focuses on colons that are used to introduce a list.

Introduce the concept
Ask the children to tell you what a colon is and if they can tell you when it might be used. Elicit examples and clarify that it is a form of punctuation. Remind children of Punctuation Unit 4 when they learned that a colon can be used to separate two clauses to introduce reasons or examples. Explain that today they will learn about colons being used to introduce a list. Write the following examples on the board to demonstrate:

- I like three sports: football, snooker and cricket.
- Dan collected things: coloured marbles, rocks and paperclips.

Ask the children in their groups to write a sentence on their mini whiteboards that uses a colon to introduce a list, and hold it up. Ask a volunteer from each group to write their sentence on the board.

Pupil practice
Pupil Book pages 45–46

Get started
Ask the children to copy and complete the lists by adding the correct punctuation. You may wish to support the children by reading each list aloud and then pausing while they discuss the punctuation needed in pairs, before asking them to copy the sentences. The first answer has been completed as an example.

Answers
Award marks for accurate use of colons only.

1. *I bought some new stationery for my return to school in September: fountain pens, pencils of different strengths, a shatterproof ruler and an eraser shaped like a snail.* [example]
2. Gran got some tasty-looking fruit at the market today: some red apples, some juicy pears, some bananas, some oranges and lots of green grapes. [1 mark]
3. Freya happily packed her little suitcase in preparation for her family holiday that summer: a bright swimsuit, a towel, cool sunglasses and her high-strength sun cream. [1 mark]
4. I have lots of things to read on the long train journey to my cousin's house: books, comics, a magazine and my tablet. [1 mark]
5. We bought lots of things for our lazy Sunday breakfast: orange juice with bits, grapefruits, fresh croissants and natural yoghurt. [1 mark]
6. The weather was really horrid last week: icily cold, very windy, really foggy and wet everywhere. [1 mark]

Try these
Ask the children to copy and complete the sentences, adding punctuation and a suitable list after the introduction. The first answer has been completed as an example. Accept any appropriate, accurately punctuated lists. They must each begin with a colon.

Example answers
1. *I own these types of shoes: trainers, sandals, pumps and boots.* [example]
2. My absolute favourite foods are: plums, apples, grapes and tomatoes. [1 mark]
3. I took some of my favourite books with me: *A Midsummer Night's Dream*, *The Borrowers* and *Ice Fairies*. [1 mark]
4. These are my favourite films of all time: *Toy Story*, *Finding Nemo* and *Mary Poppins*. [1 mark]

Punctuation Unit 5: Colons to introduce lists

5. My favourite apps on my phone at the moment are: sports, fitness and games. [1 mark]
6. I bought several small presents for my grandfather's birthday: slippers, chocolates and a CD. [1 mark]
7. The bouquet Tracey had been sent contained lots of flowers: roses, daisies, and lilies. [1 mark]
8. We heard four different instruments on the CD: violin, guitar, flute and piano. [1 mark]

Now try these

Ask the children to write their own sentence about each of the topics, making sure that they include an introduction followed by a list. They must also use the correct punctuation. The following are examples. Accept any appropriate, accurately punctuated lists. They must each begin with a colon.

Example answers

1. The ingredients for toad in the hole include: sausages, flour, milk and batter. [1 mark]
2. My favourite rides at the theme park are: the roundabout, the swings and the big wheel. [1 mark]
3. My least favourite chores around the house are: sweeping, washing-up and dusting. [1 mark]
4. Janis loves playing games, especially: Monopoly, hide and seek and football. [1 mark]
5. Playing sports is fun and I enjoy playing: netball, hockey and tennis. [1 mark]
6. I know lots of songs, but the ones I like most are sung by: Avicii, Tinie Tempah and Ed Sheeran. [1 mark]

Support, embed & challenge

Support

Work with these children in a group. Ask each child in turn to say what their three favourite footballers, favourite films, favourite characters are and so on. As each child gives their three items, work together to write a sentence about it. After a few examples, gradually encourage the children to do their own writing.

Use Punctuation Unit 5 Resource 1: I love: cake, tea and more cake to support children in becoming more confident with using an introduction before a list followed by a colon. Ask children to read the list introductions, then add a colon and write a suitable list – remembering to include commas as appropriate.

Embed

Use Punctuation Unit 5 Resource 2: Roll the dice to encourage the children to become more confident in writing the introduction to lists, including using a colon accurately. Ask children to roll a dice. The number on the dice indicates which topic they should use from their game card. Then they write an introduction and list for the given topic. They check they have used the correct punctuation then repeat the activity.

Challenge

Challenge children to collect some information from the other children in the class and make a list, using a colon to introduce it. They could survey people's favourite TV programmes, holiday destinations, toys, games, sports or hobbies. Tell them to make their list of information into a large poster that could be presented to the class.

Homework / Additional activities

Ask children to research and find an example of a list that is introduced with a colon. They could look in newspapers, leaflets and brochures, on packaging, on websites or in books.

Collins Connect: Punctuation Unit 5

Ask the children to complete Punctuation Unit 5 (see Teach → Year 5 → Vocabulary, Grammar and Punctuation → Punctuation Unit 5).

Punctuation Unit 6: Punctuating bulleted lists

Overview

English curriculum objectives
- Punctuation of bullet points to list information consistently

Treasure House resources
- Vocabulary, Grammar and Punctuation Skills Pupil Book 5, Punctuation Unit 6, pages 47–48
- Collins Connect Treasure House Vocabulary, Grammar and Punctuation Year 5, Punctuation Unit 6
- Photocopiable Punctuation Unit 6, Resource 1: Bullet it, page 103
- Photocopiable Punctuation Unit 6, Resource 2: Bullet list poster, page 104

Introduction

Teaching overview
This unit builds on the previous unit about lists to look at using bullet points to organise lists. Use the content of this unit to teach grammatical terminology and concepts so that children are able to apply them correctly to examples of real language; such as their own writing or books they have read. When modelling the teaching point, use your voice to show emphasis, intonation, tone, volume and natural speech patterns. This will help children to learn the differences between spoken and written vocabulary, grammar and punctuation.

Introduce the concept
Ask children to remind you of what they learned about punctuating lists in Punctuation Unit 5 (using a colon to introduce a list). Explain to the children that we can also use bullet points to help us organise a list so it is clear to read and understand. Explain that there are three main rules and write these on the board to demonstrate:

- If the list starts with an introduction, put a colon after it.
- Each item starts with a bullet point.
- Each item is written on a new line, one below the other.

Pupil practice
Pupil Book pages 47–48

Get started
Ask the children to copy out each sentence about bullet-pointed lists. Then they label each one 'true' or 'false'. You may wish to support the children by reading each sentence aloud and then pausing while they discuss if it is true or false, before asking them to copy the sentences.

Answers
1. *Items must be in full sentences.* false　　[example]
2. true　　[1 mark]
3. false　　[1 mark]
4. true　　[1 mark]
5. true　　[1 mark]
6. true　　[1 mark]
7. false　　[1 mark]
8. false　　[1 mark]

Try these
Ask the children to rewrite the lists as correctly punctuated, bullet-pointed lists. The first answer has been completed as an example.

Answers
Accept answers that demonstrate correctly punctuated, bullet-pointed lists. Award 3 marks for lists that follow the three main rules.

1. *These are my things to do:*
   - *make my bed,*
   - *hang up my coat,*
   - *clean my shoes.*　　[example]

Now try these
Ask the children to copy out each introduction and add a bullet-pointed list. Accept any appropriate bullet-pointed lists that follow the three main rules.

Example answers
1. I would to visit these countries when I am older:
   - Japan,
   - Greece,
   - Belgium.　　[3 marks]

2. There are lots of games you could play:
- snakes and ladders,
- Sofia's World,
- Chinese whispers. [3 marks]

3. Lots of different animals live in the jungle:
- tigers,
- chimpanzees,
- leopards. [3 marks]

Support, embed & challenge

Support
Use Punctuation Unit 6 Resource 1: Bullet it to support children to become more confident with using bullet points to write clear lists. First ask children to reread page 47 of the Pupil Book to clarify what the bullet point rules are. Then ask them to read the lists provided on the resource sheet. Then they rewrite them using correctly punctuated, bullet-pointed lists.

Answers
1. Treasures found in the loft:
- an old chest,
- dusty, leather books,
- some old clothes.

2. Mythical creatures in my book:
- a cyclops,
- a two-headed dog,
- a snake-like beast.

3. School dinners this week:
- fish fingers,
- chicken pie,
- vegetable pizza.

4. Things I am saving up my pocket money to buy:
- new trainers,
- some spinners,
- sweets.

5. Reasons I need a new notepad:
- I need to make notes,
- I forget things and need to note them down,
- to make future plans.

6. Reasons I don't want a dog:
- they smell,
- they need to be walked all the time,
- they are dirty,
- they dribble.

Embed
Use Punctuation Unit 6 Resource 2: Bullet list poster to enable children to become more confident in the rules of writing bullet-pointed lists. They need to design a poster about how to set out a bullet-pointed list, using the two lists on the resource sheet.

Challenge
Ask the children to look at the first word in each point in a range of bullet points. Ask them to explain how the words are similar.

Homework / Additional activities

Ask the children to find a selection of different bullet-pointed lists in non-fiction texts and other sources of texts, such as leaflets and posters. Ask them to look at the variety of different punctuation conventions (such as only having a full stop at the end of the last sentence or ending middle points with a semicolon).

Collins Connect: Punctuation Unit 6
Ask the children to complete Punctuation Unit 6 (see Teach → Year 5 → Vocabulary, Grammar and Punctuation → Punctuation Unit 6).

Review unit 3: Punctuation

Pupil Book pages 49–50

A. Ask the children to copy and complete the sentences, adding commas.
Answers
1. For dinner we are having mushrooms, peppers and goat's cheese. [1 mark]
2. I am going to invite Rauhan, Emma and Hattie to my birthday party. [1 mark]
3. At the supermarket we bought cooking oil, soup and bread. [1 mark]
4. In my jewellery box I have a necklace, a bracelet and my old watch. [1 mark]
5. For my camping trip I need to pack a sleeping bag, an extra blanket and a change of clothes. [1 mark]

B. Ask the children to look at each pair of phrases and copy out the phrases that use hyphens correctly.
Answers
1. a) the deep-fried fish [1 mark]
2. a) a part-time job [1 mark]
3. b) the beautiful red bow [1 mark]
4. a) the high-rise flats [1 mark]
5. b) a soft flowery cushion [1 mark]

C. Ask the children to copy out the sentences, adding some extra information in parenthesis.
Answers will vary.
Example answers
1. We are going (supposedly today!) to the science museum. [1 mark]
2. Our new family car – or you could call it a truck – is red. [1 mark]
3. Aunt Jean (who lives in Wales) is baking me a birthday cake. [1 mark]
4. We went for a bike ride – a very long one – through the forest. [1 mark]
5. The library (on West Street) is due to close early this afternoon. [1 mark]

D. Ask children to copy and complete the sentences, adding a colon, semicolon or dash between the two independent clauses.
Example answers
1. Our teacher had an idea: we could go on a nature walk. [1 mark]
2. Imran cheered; he loved being outdoors. [1 mark]
3. He chose the blue umbrella – I chose the red one. [1 mark]
4. Later we had a pop quiz – I won! [1 mark]
5. We might do it again on Friday; I'll be better prepared next time. [1 mark]

E. Ask the children to copy and complete the sentences, adding punctuation and a suitable list after the introduction. Answers will vary.
Example answers
1. Types of T-shirts I own: long-sleeved, short-sleeved, patterned and plain. [1 mark]
2. Places I like to visit in the holidays are: the museum, the library, the forest and the beach. [1 mark]
3. My favourite sports are: cricket, hockey and rugby. [1 mark]

F. Ask the children to copy out each introduction and add a bullet-pointed list after it. Answers will vary.
Example answers
1. There is a lot of wildlife under the sea:
   - turtles
   - fish
   - urchins
   - sharks [3 marks]
2. There are lots of activities to take part in at school:
   - running club
   - swimming club
   - art club
   - choir [3 marks]
3. These are things you could buy at a grocer's store:
   - cabbage
   - peppers
   - onions [3 marks]

Vocabulary Unit 1 Resource 1

Noun phrase spotter

Which part of speech are these? Put a tick in the right column.

	Noun phrase	Adjective	Prepositional phrase
stone			
in the paper bag			
a bag			
with the dusty cover			
the horse			
with silver buckles			
on top of the hill			
the book			
golden			
ancient			
his sweets			
leather			
with the long mane			
chewy			
a castle			

Put together a noun, an adjective and a prepositional phrase from the chart to create four different noun phrases.

_____

_____

_____

_____

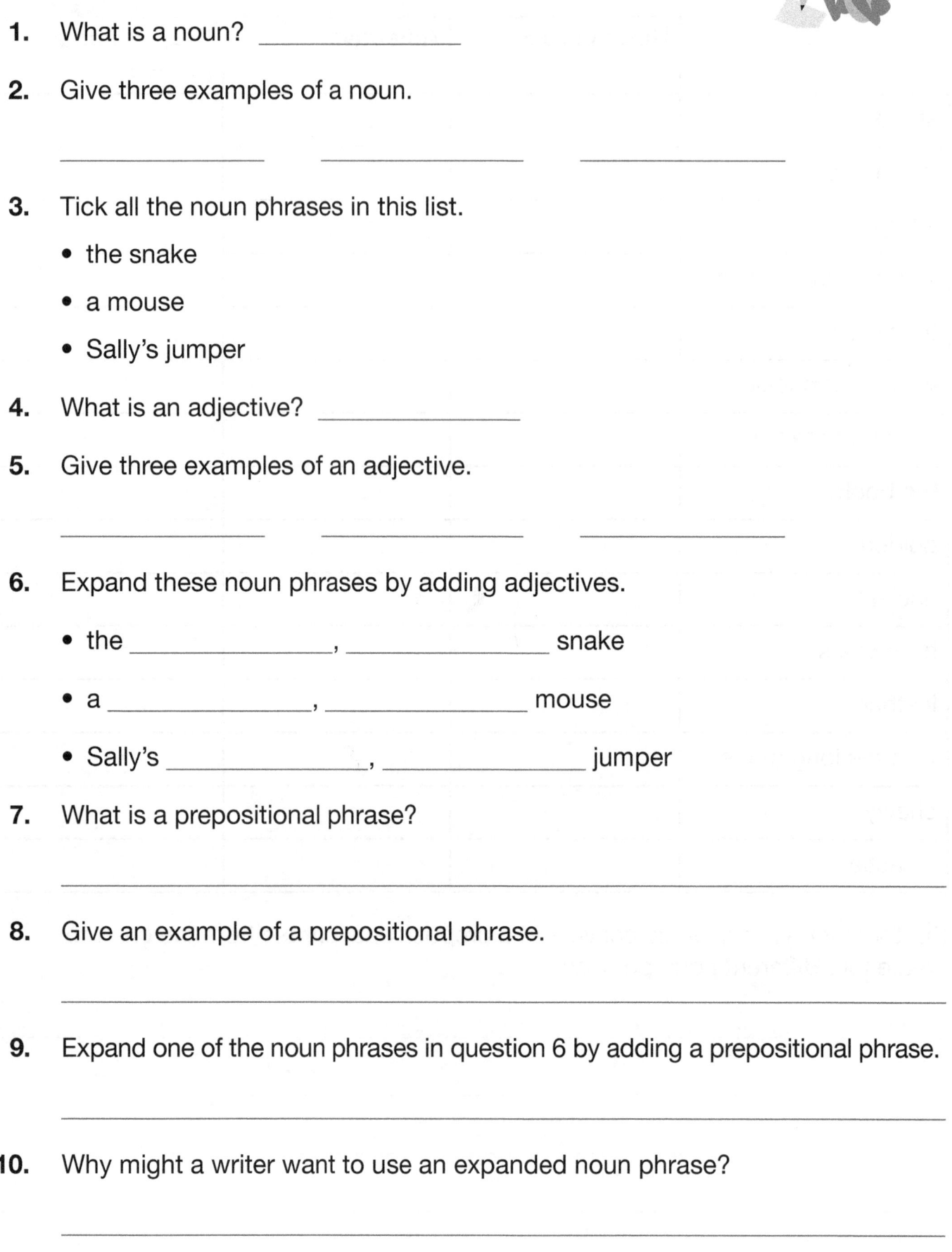

Vocabulary Unit 1 Resource 2

Noun phrase quiz

How well do you know noun phrases? Let's find out:

1. What is a noun? _____

2. Give three examples of a noun.

   _____   _____   _____

3. Tick all the noun phrases in this list.
   - the snake
   - a mouse
   - Sally's jumper

4. What is an adjective? _____

5. Give three examples of an adjective.

   _____   _____   _____

6. Expand these noun phrases by adding adjectives.
   - the _____, _____ snake
   - a _____, _____ mouse
   - Sally's _____, _____ jumper

7. What is a prepositional phrase?

   _____

8. Give an example of a prepositional phrase.

   _____

9. Expand one of the noun phrases in question 6 by adding a prepositional phrase.

   _____

10. Why might a writer want to use an expanded noun phrase?

    _____

Vocabulary Unit 2 Resource 1

Verb word search

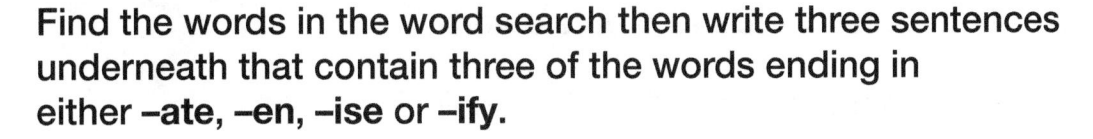

Find the words in the word search then write three sentences underneath that contain three of the words ending in either **–ate, –en, –ise** or **–ify**.

Words to find

assassinate	darken	authorise	glorify
captivate	frighten	advertise	intensify
motivate	loosen	computerise	falsify

a	u	t	h	o	r	i	s	e	d	c
s	d	k	y	l	n	g	g	w	k	o
s	a	c	f	o	f	a	l	e	q	m
a	r	t	l	o	d	j	o	h	f	p
s	k	m	r	s	b	v	r	m	r	u
s	e	o	i	e	l	m	i	e	i	t
i	n	t	e	n	s	i	f	y	g	e
n	h	i	u	i	z	f	y	a	h	r
a	d	v	e	r	t	i	s	e	t	i
t	c	a	p	t	i	v	a	t	e	s
e	a	t	o	n	c	j	b	p	n	e
g	s	e	x	f	a	l	s	i	f	y

Cut out the words in the list above and the list below. Pair up the words.

Tell a partner how the spelling and meaning of each word has changed.

captive	computer	motive	dark
author	advert	glory	fright
intense	assassin	loose	false

Vocabulary Unit 2 Resource 2

Verb generator

Add –ise, –ate, –en or –ify to these words to create a verb.

Remember: you might need to remove letters from the original word before adding the correct suffix.

white		loose	
illustration		emphasis	
bright		estimation	
real		note	
maximum		motive	
intense		deep	
operation		apology	
just		solid	
beauty		straight	
investigation		terror	
deaf		calculation	
special		symbol	

Vocabulary Unit 3A Resource 1

Retake and mistake

Sort the words into the correct column depending on which prefix you can add to the word. Some words may be placed in both columns.

Write the word, with its prefix, in the correct column.

Words to sort
build   heat   write   entered   advise   use   take   place   open
judge   pay   direct   estimate   behave   appear   heard   fortune
considered   fit   inform   place   understand   direct   apply   activate
spell   construe   communicate   play   treat

re–	mis–

Vocabulary Unit 3A Resource 2

Replacing words

Add **re–** or **mis–** to the words in the box.

Use the words you've created to complete the sentences.

Watch out: some words can use either prefix but only one option will fit the sentence.

| build   direct   write   judged   place   advise   pay   use |

1. We will need to _____ the broken tiles too.

2. If you _____ them, they will end up at the wrong location.

3. If you want to borrow that money I will need you to _____ it next week.

4. I think you've _____ the new teacher. Give her another chance.

5. You'd be better to ask an expert because I don't want to _____ you.

6. The construction workers will try to _____ the wall within the next week.

7. Don't _____ this time by mucking around: work hard and finish the job.

8. My story was so bad I had to _____ it.

Vocabulary Unit 3B Resource 1

Choosing over–, de– or dis–

Add **over–**, **de–** or **dis–** to the words in the box. Write the new word in the correct column.

If you can add more than one prefix, do so.

Words to sort
load   able   code   activate   honour   appoint   approve   fill   obey
qualify   rail   value   connect   estimate   forest   congest   statement
eat   cook   agreed   scribe   fuse   able   integrate   count   pleased
hydrate   bone   frost   react   crowding   paid   order   cipher   trust

over–	de–	dis–

Vocabulary Unit 3B Resource 2

Please disable that toy!

Add **over–**, **dis–** or **de–** to the words in the box.

Use the words you've created to complete the sentences.

| rail | ice | filled | code | forestation | estimate | able | appoint |

1. We had to leave early to _____ the car.

2. If you guess, you might _____ how much you need.

3. If I can _____ Dad's handwriting, I will tell you what his note says.

4. We _____ our shopping bags and they broke in the car park.

5. Mum took the batteries out of the noisy toy to _____ it.

6. I don't want to _____ you, but the match is cancelled today.

7. We saw the train _____ just outside of the station.

8. Many scientists are worried about the _____ of the Amazon Rainforest.

Grammar Unit 1 Resource 1

Formal or informal?

Colour the boxes in the grid that are examples of informal language. How many can you find?

That's so cool!	Please do not touch that!	What you up to?	Just hanging around.
Don't you hate it when that happens?	What about Tuesday?	Mmm, not sure.	I am so looking forward to seeing this show.
I'm writing to enquire if you have a vacancy on Friday 1 June.	Had a good time?	I will need to check with Margo.	I am sorry, please can you repeat that?
I understand that you have been very busy.	How does 4 p.m. sound?	Who else will be there?	Ahhh – so cute!
Friday is fine with me.	I dunno.	Sounds like a good plan.	Yes, that would be convenient for me.

© HarperCollins*Publishers* 2017

73

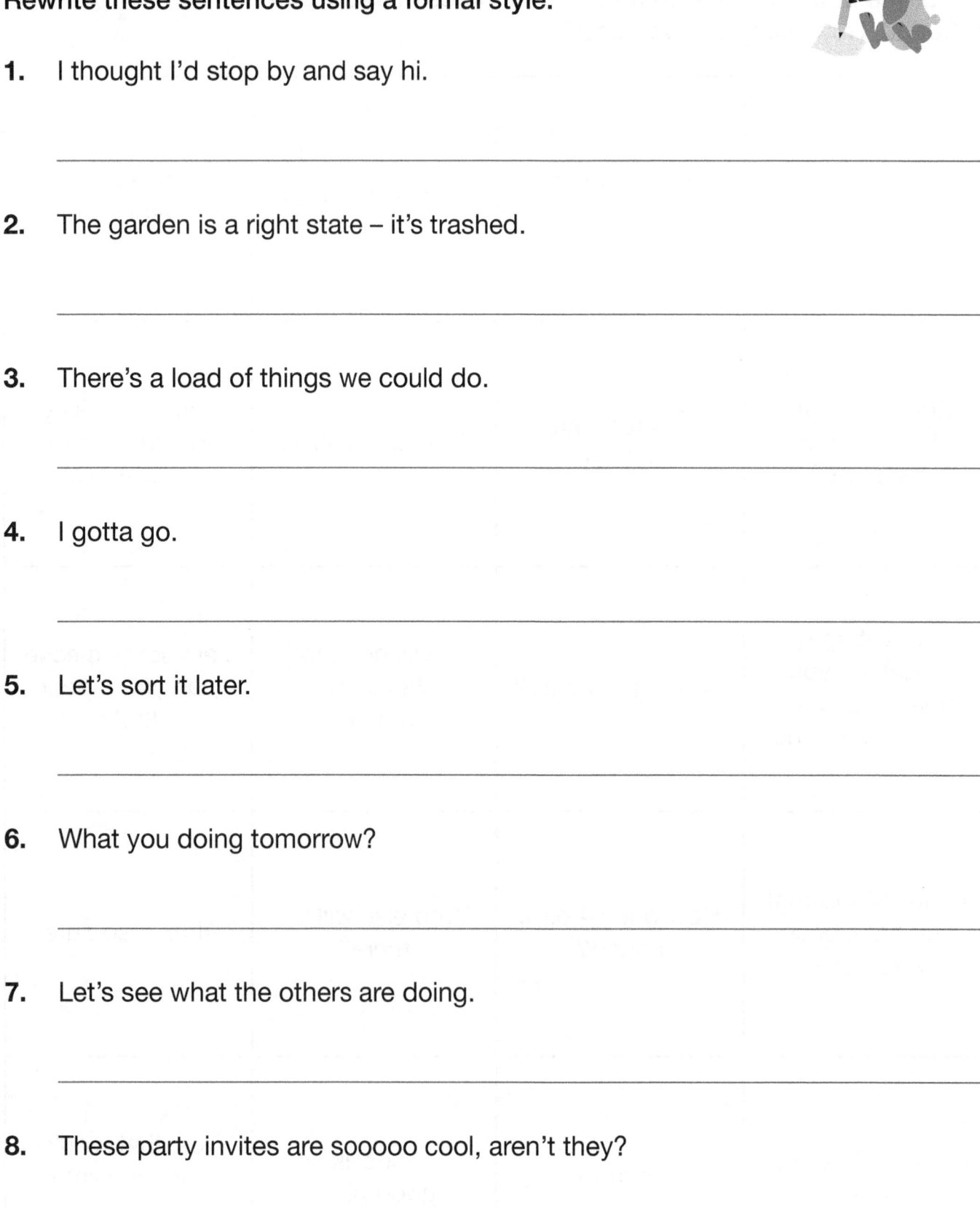

Grammar Unit 1 Resource 2

Watch your language

Rewrite these sentences using a formal style.

1. I thought I'd stop by and say hi.

2. The garden is a right state – it's trashed.

3. There's a load of things we could do.

4. I gotta go.

5. Let's sort it later.

6. What you doing tomorrow?

7. Let's see what the others are doing.

8. These party invites are sooooo cool, aren't they?

Grammar Unit 2A Resource 1

Definitely maybe

Find the adverbs of possibility in the word search.

Choose words from the list to complete the sentences.

Words to find

perhaps   maybe   possibly   definitely   certainly

surely   rarely   occasionally   generally   usually

o	c	c	a	s	i	o	n	a	l	l	y
e	q	e	m	h	y	p	a	f	h	y	d
p	e	r	h	a	p	s	b	o	c	x	e
o	n	t	f	l	u	u	s	g	u	i	f
s	m	a	y	b	e	r	q	k	w	t	i
s	a	i	k	s	m	e	v	d	u	k	n
i	j	n	n	p	z	l	e	j	s	r	i
b	o	l	a	w	l	y	l	j	u	a	t
l	i	y	u	b	d	z	d	g	a	r	e
y	y	i	t	r	w	z	g	x	l	e	l
f	v	e	g	e	n	e	r	a	l	l	y
h	s	c	o	r	p	t	x	q	y	y	r

1. At the weekend we _____ go swimming.

2. I am _____ going to do my homework as soon as I get home.

3. When Saul and Joseph play tennis, Saul _____ wins.

4. _____ we'll be able to go to the cinema on Saturday.

© HarperCollins*Publishers* 2017   75

Grammar Unit 2A Resource 2

Unquestionably and undoubtedly

Work with a partner. Cut the page in half to have one board each. Take turns to roll a dice. Match the number on your dice to a number on the board. Use that word to say or write a sentence.

1. perhaps	2. possibly	3. certainly
4. rarely	5. unquestionably	6. undoubtedly

---

1. maybe	2. definitely	3. surely
4. occasionally	5. absolutely	6. generally

© HarperCollins*Publishers* 2017

Grammar Unit 2B Resource 1

We should and we could

Choose a modal verb from the box to complete each sentence.
Try to choose a different word each time.

can   could   may   might   must   shall   should   will   would

1. Tomas _____ come to our house after school if he likes.

2. Pirrita _____ do her homework before she plays on the computer.

3. The weather _____ be hot tomorrow.

4. When you have finished, you _____ go out and play.

5. Suki _____ arrive at about 6 p.m.

6. Joseph _____ like to be a musician when he is older.

7. You _____ have another biscuit when you get back.

8. We _____ go and visit Uncle Robert on our way to the campsite.

Grammar Unit 2B Resource 2

I certainly might

Write a reply to each of these questions. Your reply must include at least one modal verb and at least one adverb of possibility.

Modal verbs

| can | could | may | might | must | ought | shall | should | will | would |

Adverbs of possibility

| perhaps | maybe | possibly | definitely | certainly |
| surely | rarely | occasionally | generally | usually |

1. Is Sandra coming to your party?

2. Where are you going on holiday?

3. What is that book like?

4. Are you going to netball after school?

5. What will you do after school today?

6. What would you like to do when you are older?

7. Will you celebrate your next birthday with a party?

8. When will you visit your relatives?

Grammar Unit 3A Resource 1

Relative clause match

Cut up the grid to make cards.

Sort the cards into two piles – one for main clauses and the second for relative clauses.

Then match the relative clauses to the main clauses to make sentences.

Sandra is my riding instructor	My uncle is the man
that leads to the supermarket.	I love winter mornings
whose successes are always in the news.	that I have been saving up to buy.
I have a new plan	This is the swimming pool
who only talks about horses.	I went down the road
Football practice finishes at seven o'clock	Lewis is an excellent golfer
This is the skateboard	that are from my mum.
Today is the last day of term	Paris is the city
Look at these messages	when there is frost all over the grass.
where Mum brings us on Saturday mornings.	whose hair is slicked over to one side.
where you can see the Eiffel Tower.	which means a lie-in tomorrow morning.
which involves working extra hard.	when it starts to get dark.

Grammar Unit 3A Resource 2

Miss it out?

Read these sentences.

Find the relative clause and underline the relative pronoun.

Decide if the sentence would work if the relative pronoun was missed out. If so, cross it out.

1. There's the lady whom I told you about.

2. Sunny, who was running late, ran as fast as he could for the bus.

3. There's the bus that we need to catch.

4. We found shop where Mum had left her purse.

5. Where's the present that we bought for Sacha?

6. Find the book that needs to go back to the library.

7. Terry thanked Mrs Parker when she returned his football.

8. That's the film that I want you to take me to.

9. Dad dropped Daisy off at the pool where the gala was taking place.

10. That's the set that I want for my birthday.

Grammar Unit 3B Resource 1

It's all relative

Read the sentences, write a relative clause, and add any missing commas.

1. That boy _____ was on the news.

2. The table _____ is falling apart.

3. Yesterday I was fast asleep when _____.

4. My neighbour has put up a fence _____.

5. I am going to visit the games shop _____.

6. Yesterday _____ we went to the skateboard park.

7. In a room at the end of the corridor _____ I found a dusty chest.

8. Mum put Paul's shoes _____ in the bin.

9. The shop _____ is shut.

10. It was nearly 1 p.m. _____.

Grammar Unit 3B Resource 2

Add a clause

Add a relative clause to the middle of these sentences. Remember to add commas around the relative clause.

1. Granny took us to our favourite café.

2. On Friday we are going ice-skating.

3. Blackpool is on the northwest coast of England.

4. Richard and Fiona have bought a new car.

5. Dad's computer is broken.

6. Paddington is a busy train station in London.

7. Tokyo is a long way from here.

8. Kieran's dog has big floppy ears.

Grammar Unit 4 Resource 1

Finding connections

Colour the boxes in the grid that are examples of linking words and phrases. How many can you find?

in the beginning	paragraph	because	emails
sentence	after that	because of this	connection
link	reader	now	so
next	but	understand	as a result
finally	needed	popular	efforts

Grammar Unit 4 Resource 2

Making it flow

Complete these sentences by adding connecting adverbials or conjunctions to create a paragraph about a visit to a theatre show.

1. _____, we checked our bags to make sure we had everything we needed.

2. _____, we all bundled into the minibus ready to set off.

3. It was a hot journey, _____ we had plenty of cool drinks with us.

4. _____, we arrived at the theatre and made our way inside.

5. We joined the queue _____ we needed to hand over our tickets.

6. We found our seats _____.

7. _____, the show started.

8. We had a great seats _____ we could see the stage really clearly.

9. _____, we put our coats on and headed back to the minibus.

10. _____, we arrived home and crashed out in our beds.

Grammar Unit 5A Resource 1

Last month at the farm

Read the adverbials in the chart and tick to show whether each is an adverbial of time, or an adverbial of place.

Adverbials	Of time?	Of place?
1. Last month		
2. After		
3. Up the hill		
4. For two days		
5. Under the tree		
6. On Thursday		
7. At the farm		
8. In the countryside		
9. By the following week		
10. Since Monday		

Grammar Unit 5A Resource 2

When did that happen?

Rewrite and expand these sentences by adding an adverbial of time.

1. Peter went to the park.

2. Madeleine cleared out the house.

3. We went for a long walk.

4. Harry arrived at the hospital.

5. Shyan travelled to Pakistan.

6. Esther hid the presents.

7. Bryan hired a boat.

8. Hikmat worked through the night.

9. The children laughed.

10. The family are moving house.

Grammar Unit 5B Resource 1

Over the hill and far away

Cut out the cards in the grid.

Sort the cards into two piles – those that are adverbials of place (where) and those that are adverbials of manner (how).

up the hill	patiently	beautifully	back
quickly	under a tree	around	anxiously
eastwards	carefully	clumsily	at the farm
bravely	in the city	sideways	everywhere
nearby	greedily	at the end of the road	over there

© HarperCollins Publishers 2017

Grammar Unit 5B Resource 2

Where did he go?

Rewrite and expand these sentences by adding an adverbial of time.

1. Dawn keeps rabbits.

2. Salim is starting a new job.

3. We went for an adventure.

4. Aunty Seema is going to live abroad.

5. Olivia looked for her pencil.

6. The boys watched the hockey match.

7. Everyone ran as fast as they could.

8. The butterflies were flying above our heads.

9. Alan went to the race track.

10. There is a famous monument.

Grammar Unit 5C Resource 1

Sentences with style

Roll a dice. Make up a sentence containing the adverbial of manner in the square that matches the number on the dice.

1. anxiously	2. ferociously	3. genuinely
4. superficially	5. beautifully	6. graciously

Now try these phrases.

1. without a doubt	2. like a baby	3. with style
4. like a rocket	5. as fast as she could	6. very slowly

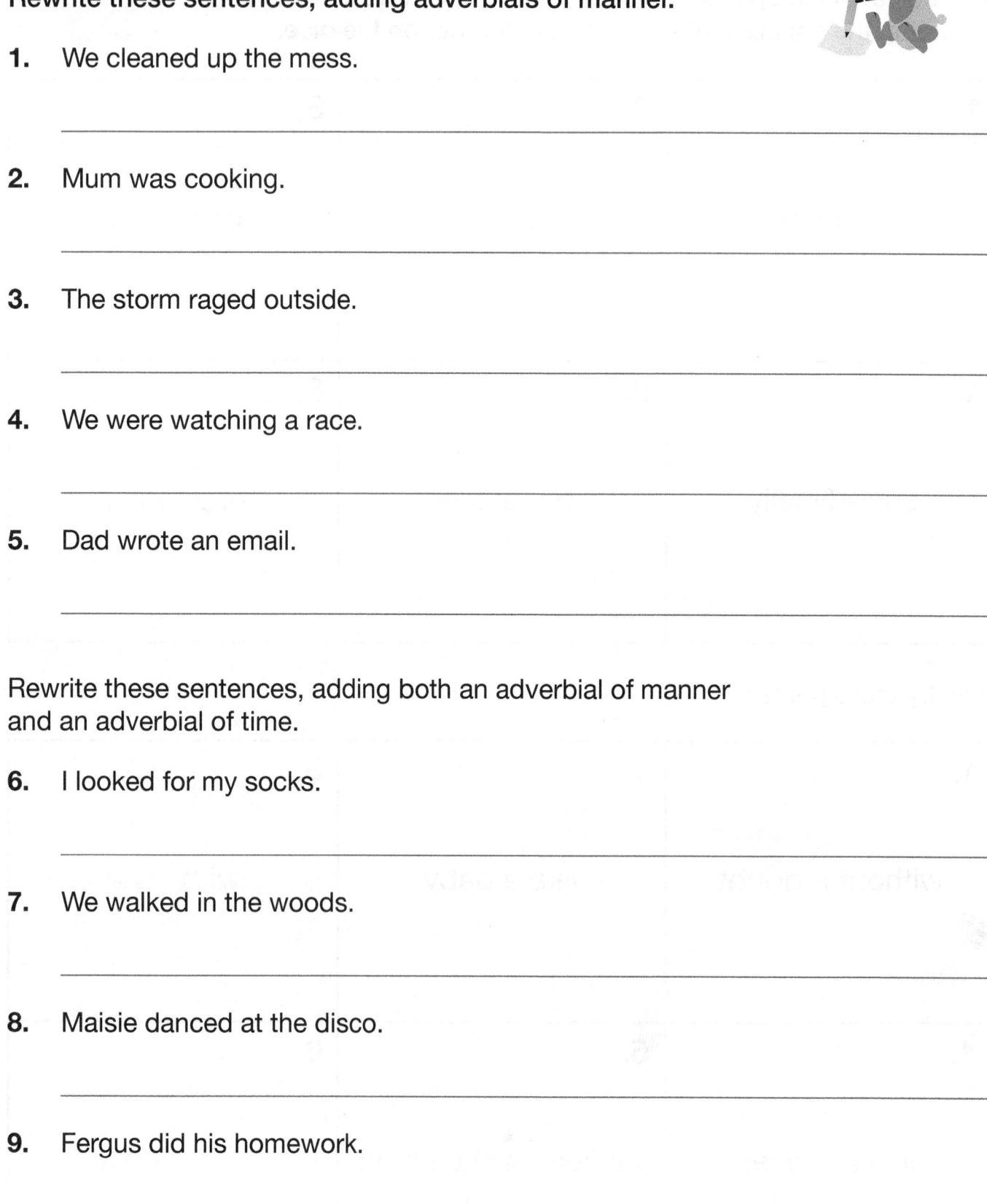

Grammar Unit 5C Resource 2

How did she do that?

Rewrite these sentences, adding adverbials of manner.

1. We cleaned up the mess.

2. Mum was cooking.

3. The storm raged outside.

4. We were watching a race.

5. Dad wrote an email.

Rewrite these sentences, adding both an adverbial of manner and an adverbial of time.

6. I looked for my socks.

7. We walked in the woods.

8. Maisie danced at the disco.

9. Fergus did his homework.

Grammar Unit 5D Resource 1

Adverbials of number game

Roll a dice. Move squares. Follow the instructions on the squares.

Make a sentence using 'always' Score 2 points	Move back 1 space	Make a sentence using 'secondly' Score 2 points	Move forwards 3 spaces
Move forwards 3 spaces			Make a sentence using 'four times a week' Score 2 points
Make a sentence using 'seldom' Score 2 points			Move back 1 space
Move back 1 space			Make a sentence using 'twice a day' Score 2 points
Make a sentence using 'lastly' Score 2 points			Move forward 3 spaces
Move forwards 3 spaces			Make a sentence using 'first' Score 2 points
Make a sentence using 'three times' Score 2 points	Move back 1 space	Make a sentence using 'third' Score 2 points	**Start here**

Grammar Unit 5D Resource 2

How often?

Rewrite and expand these sentences by adding two adverbial phrases: an adverbial phrase of number and an adverbial phrase of manner or place.

1. The milkman delivers the milk and juice.

2. I visit my cousins.

3. I can't wait.

4. Teresa bakes cakes.

5. I like to go shopping.

6. I clean the car.

7. The birds fly over the rooftops.

8. The caterpillars eat the leaves.

9. Adrienne went to the hairdressers.

10. They finished building the bridge.

Punctuation Unit 1 Resource 1

Comma quiz

Check your knowledge of using commas by answering these questions.

1. Commas can help to make the meanings of sentences clearer. — **true / false**

2. Commas show small breaks or pauses between words, phrases or clauses. — **true / false**

3. Commas should not be used in lists. — **true / false**

4. Commas can be used after fronted adverbials. — **true / false**

5. Commas should not be used either side of a relative clause. — **true / false**

6. You can use a comma instead of a full stop at the end of a sentence. — **true / false**

Add commas to these sentences.

1. For dinner we ate spaghetti bolognaise garlic bread mozzarella sticks and tomatoes.

2. After a while we were all ready to go home.

3. The gentleman whose dogs we were walking wanted them home for teatime.

Punctuation Unit 1 Resource 2

Commas galore

Add commas to the correct places in these sentences.

1. Mum says I must put my laundry away tidy my desk and take my empty cups to the kitchen.

2. Today we baked gingerbread biscuits chocolate chip cookies shortbread and a Victoria sponge.

3. At the car show I saw a funny red sports car a huge green tractor a flashy blue motorbike and a silver Rolls Royce.

4. Next Thursday we are moving house.

5. After a very long time away the giant finally returned home.

6. With a sudden flash the skies turned black and rain lashed down.

7. My friend who is an excellent writer has nearly finished writing a whole book.

8. It all started when a strange parcel that was small and rectangular arrived in the post.

9. My job which was terribly important was to protect the treasure map at all costs.

10. I am going to make us a snack of ice cream soda and crisps.

Punctuation Unit 2 Resource 1

Compound adjective generator

Cut out the cards in the grid. Jumble them up and place them on the table. Pair them up to create as many compound adjectives as you can.

Choose three of your compound adjectives to use in a sentence. Remember to use a hyphen to connect the parts of your compound adjective.

middle	quick	kind	good	long
aged	witted	hearted	looking	lasting
never	mouth	slow	far	time
ending	watering	moving	reaching	saving
world	brightly	forward	absent	well
famous	lit	thinking	minded	educated
short	old	well	twenty	part
haired	fashioned	behaved	paged	time
short	quick	three	fire	long
sighted	drying	legged	eating	necked

© HarperCollins*Publishers* 2017

95

Punctuation Unit 2 Resource 2

The super-useful hyphen

In each of these sentences one or two hyphens are missing.
Add them in.

1. Sir George ran away from the fire breathing dragon as fast as he could.

2. Corry jumped into the ice cold water.

3. I have got to babysit my irritating four year old cousin this afternoon.

4. The garden had become overgrown in the warm, wet mid June weather.

5. My great grandfather is ninety six years old.

6. The sea was a stormy grey green and the wind whipped around the already cold tourists.

7. Mina ate the day old sandwiches and drank the funny tasting milk.

8. Nile felt silly in his too small jumper and too short trousers.

9. There are many strange looking creatures at the bottom of the deepest part of the ocean.

10. We ate ice creams at the beach and put T-shirts on our already burned arms.

Punctuation Unit 3 Resource 1

Parenthesis practice

Read the sentences. Underline the parenthesis and add punctuation marks.

1. A magazine article written in 2013 revealed the secrets of the author's greatest book.

2. The girl Sally Anne decided she would try to be more helpful in future.

3. He ran and hid before anyone had noticed he was gone under the stairwell.

4. The teacher who was very clever tried the children's test and failed it.

5. Kieran told his aunt who was shocked about the discovery.

6. The children with the help of Mr Edge the caretaker set off towards the wooded area.

7. It had been a long day which was normal for Wednesdays but it was nearly home time.

8. Finally at just after 5 p.m. Heidi called.

9. The forest with its collection of Nordic trees was spookily inviting.

10. The cave that they had been searching for all day was finally visible in the distance.

Punctuation Unit 3 Resource 2

Commas, brackets and dashes

Rewrite these sentences, adding extra information in parenthesis.

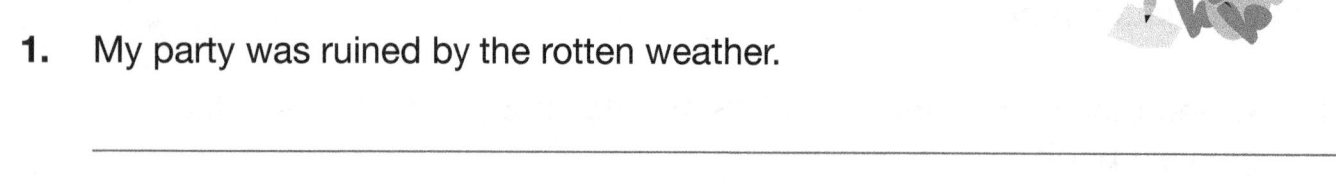

1. My party was ruined by the rotten weather.

2. The butterfly farm was experiencing a crisis.

3. She knew that tomorrow was going to be hard work.

4. I am planning my next holiday.

5. The horses jumped the fence and escaped.

6. The storm winds lashed at the window.

7. We snuggled up under extra blankets to keep warm.

8. Verity stayed up extra late.

9. The author's new book was due to be released in the morning.

10. The shops had stacked their shelves sky high.

Punctuation Unit 4 Resource 1

Colon – semicolon – dash

Test your knowledge.

1. When would you use a colon between independent clauses?

   _____

2. When would you use a semicolon between independent clauses?

   _____

3. When would you use a dash between independent clauses?

   _____

Now add colons, semicolons or dashes between the independent clauses in the sentences.

1. Kasey had a plan she wanted to look in the loft.

2. Mum frowned the loft could be dangerous.

3. Dad got the ladder out Kasey got her torch.

4. Kasey's torch wouldn't turn on it had run out of battery.

5. Dad fetched new batteries Kasey was gone!

6. The weather had turned sunny Kasey wanted to make the most of it.

Punctuation Unit 4 Resource 2

After the dash

Complete these sentences by adding a suitable independent clause.

1. He left the house early: _____

2. The traffic was heavy; _____

3. The sky was still dark – _____

4. He decided to take a detour: _____

5. It was a bad idea; _____

6. He tried to phone home; _____

7. An owl landed on a nearby fence post – _____

8. He thought of a new plan: _____

9. The sun rose in the distance: _____

10. He knew everything was going to be OK; _____

Punctuation Unit 5 Resource 1

I love: cake, tea and more cake

Read the list introductions. Then add a colon and write a suitable list after each introduction – remembering to include commas as appropriate.

1. Types of birds I see in my garden

2. My favourite snacks

3. Things I carry in my school bag

4. Books I have read this year

5. Places I would love to go

6. Things I did when I was younger

7. What my family does to celebrate special occasions

8. Animals you might see at the aquarium

Punctuation Unit 5 Resource 2

Roll the dice

Roll a dice. The number on the dice indicates which topic you should use from the game card. Write an introduction and list for the given topic. Check you have used the correct punctuation then repeat the activity.

1. pets	2. fruit	3. clothing
4. holidays	5. sports	6. hobbies

Punctuation Unit 6 Resource 1

Bullet it

Rewrite these lists as correctly punctuated, bullet-pointed lists.

1. Treasures we found in the loft: an old chest, dusty leather books, some old clothes.

2. Mythical creatures in my book: a cyclops, a two-headed dog, a snake-like beast.

3. School dinners this week: fish fingers, chicken pie, vegetable pizza.

4. Things I am saving up my pocket money to buy: new trainers, some spinners, sweets.

5. Reasons I need a new notepad: I need to make notes, I forget things and need to note them down, to make future plans.

6. Reasons I don't want a dog: they smell, they need to be walked all the time, they are dirty and they dribble.

Punctuation Unit 6 Resource 2

Bullet list poster

Use these two sets of bullet points to make a poster about how to set out a bullet list. Circle features of bullet lists and label them.

Today's tasty snacks are:

- apple slices
- carrot sticks
- bread sticks
- orange juice

In the autumn term, the Year 6 students will be going to the Windfall Adventure Centre. Over the course of the week we will be:

- learning to sail on the lake and having a picnic on an island in the lake
- climbing on a purpose-built climbing wall
- having a go at fencing and archery
- making fires and cooking our dinner outside
- sleeping outside under the stars